Memories Unlocked

Memories Unlocked

Short stories, poems and anecdotes from SWit'CH

Copyright and Ordering

First Printing: 2020
ISBN: 9798570919617

Swinton Writers in t'Critchley Hub
Age UK Critchley Community Hub
75 Chorley Road
Swinton
Manchester
M27 4AF
United Kingdom

Web site: http://www.switchwriters.btck.co.uk/

Ordering Information:

Published with Amazon KDP. Available through Amazon and good book distributors or directly from Age UK at the address above or
E-mail: switchswinton@gmail.com

Contents

Dedication Audrey Edwards

'Frugal and profound' was how our SWITCH colleague, Audrey

Edwards described her writing style. She had a ready wit and the gift of reflecting equal measures of pathos and humour in her submissions.

Although a talented crafts-lady and a former amateur actress, she had not put pen to paper until 2018 so although she was not out of her depth this was how she felt and only produced brief articles. Encouraged by her fellow scribblers, she was beginning to produce fine pieces of a longer length.

Having a rich and melodious voice, Audrey was also a valued volunteer, through SWITCH, as a reader for 'Newspapers for the Blind' and became a regular contributor.

Sadly, she died suddenly on 1 August 2020.

The products of her hand and voice remain with us as a lasting warm memory. One of her specialities was creating Teddy Bears. It is, therefore, apt and our great pleasure to include her last piece of writing, 'Who Will Buy Me?' in this collection.

Who Will Buy Me?

Take a look at where I've ended up -
On a second-hand stall.
Has all the love they showered on me
Meant zilch, nothing at all?
I've got my eye on a cutie over there,
She's not much to look at, unless you're a bear.
Her eyes are just buttons
And her bottom is baggy,
Her stuffing's come out
And she's looking all saggy.
But she has that certain je ne sais quoi?
Don't you think she could be a star?

Who will buy me? I'm worried about that.
This pretty girl in the sky blue hat?
Or a kind old man who wants company for his cat?
A sweet and gentle octogenarian,
A mung-bean-munching vegetarian,
Or a colourful dreadlocked Rastafarian?

Oh, please, not this one,
She will kiss me all day long,
And every time she picks me up
She will break out into song.
This one looks nice,
She will sit me on her knee,
And every day at three o'clock
There'll be honey scones for tea

Audrey Edwards

Balaclavas, Coats and Shoes

CHRIS VICKERS

I vividly recall my first day at primary school, getting ready and a slight nervousness emanating back and forth between Mum and me. I remember that first walk, with hundreds to follow, cutting through the back alleys, me running ahead, as usual, crossing a couple of minor roads, before Mum clutching my hand tightly as we reached the busy main road in front of the school. She ensuring the traffic had stopped on both sides before guiding me over.

I think back to entering school for the first time, Mum briefly involved in adult conversation, before us both being escorted to my classroom and meeting my cohorts, who were already gathered and staring at this latecomer intently. One boy, William, especially stuck in my memory as he was taller than the rest and was, I instinctively realised 'different.'

I quickly settled into school life and loved it. I enjoyed learning and the routines of the classroom. Even more welcome were the playtimes. Playing football on the concrete concourse using jumpers for goals; being chased by George who had a crude false arm which he whirled around whanging any kids impertinent to him. The girls were always separate from the lads: walking around the playground in pairs deep in conversation; playing hopscotch, or doing handstands against the school wall.

My instinct regarding William proved to be accurate. He had innate musical talents and transferred to Chetham's School of Music as soon as he was allowed to, much to the relief of his Mother who had confided to Mum that he wouldn't survive in the rough and tumble of mainstream education. I greatly hope that he thrived at Chetham's and fulfilled whatever gifts he possessed.

As for me I thrived at my beloved primary school becoming besotted by football and also enjoying sprinting on the 100 yard track painted at one end of the play area. Saturday mornings were taken over playing soccer against local schools such as Light Oaks, Ordsall and Clarendon. Tremendous! In the winter, returning home to a hot bath and either a piece of warm toast or, occasionally and even better, a 'dip butty'.

The only cloud on the horizon was when the bus arrived at the school gates and we boarded en route to Frederick Road baths. Deep dread invaded me on these occasions. The sinister Victorian building oozed menace on the outside. Freezing cold on entering and accompanied with the awful, pungent smell of chlorine that took the breath away. We got changed in damp cubicles with cloth curtains, usually hanging off, and were then lined up along the side of the pool, staring into the evil, freezing, chemically-treated water. Through fear my breathing was shallow…'please God don't make me jump in!'…they never did but I hated having to put my face in the water and always struggled to get my breath.

Another memory pervades of an event outside the school gates. I must have been about seven I assume when that rite of passage inheriting a sibling's bike occurs. In this case a beautiful shiny little red number. I recall sitting on the cycle as Dad adjusted the saddle so that only my toes reached the ground when my bottom was in the seat. This didn't seem at all right to my mind, surely you should be able to place both feet flatly on the ground. Anyway, adjustments completed it was time for my maiden bike ride. Off we set from outside our front gate Dad holding the rear of the saddle providing stability and gently pushing to build momentum. Concentrating fully I eventually heard his somewhat detached voice urging me to keep pedalling and felt both elated and terrified at the same time. As I progressed up the road a feeling of serenity briefly overtook me. This cycling game wasn't so difficult after all!

All of a sudden Dad's tone changed: 'Stop pedalling. Pull on your brakes' as I sped on up the road. After that initial push Dad had remained near our house admiring my efficiency I guessed. Now, however, I was hurtling towards the T Junction with Acresfield Road, a feeder road for the busy A6. Serenity was replaced with cold fear and sheer panic. I had no idea how to brake, turn right or left or indeed anything other than hurtle forwards. Luckily even at that age I intuited that riding across the T Junction was not something I should do and Dad realising that pulling on the brakes would send me flying over them in all probability changed his tune to: 'turn round, turn round' and, at hearing this I yanked the handlebars right and went careering across our road, riding head first into the dentist's wall at the top of the road, with Dad running as fast as he could to ensure that I was still *compos mentis*.

That would not be the only time in my life that I ran headlong into brick walls, mostly due to my impetuosity and urge to 'get things done'.

In those early school days winters were properly cold affairs and to counter them Mum dressed my sister and I in black gabardine raincoats and grey woollen gloves. Nice and cosy. However, I also suffered the indignity of having to wear a grey knitted balaclava. A ghastly creation that caused battles royal getting it on as it always seemed to go on back to front leaving me gasping for air. The raincoats were hideous but I am unable to articulate my loathing of the balaclava.

I remember one day going to play football with the lads on Duchy Road playing fields and my gabardine raincoat was laid down as one of the goalposts. At the end of the kickabout, hot and sweaty, I nonchalantly told my mate, Norman that he could keep the coat and set off homewards, tired but happy. As soon as I entered the kitchen via the backdoor Mum turned to see me and instantly said:

'Where's your coat?'

Me: 'I gave it to Norman.'

That was the first time I actually saw someone turn apoplectic, with figurative smoke coming from her ears and forming speech bubbles above her head.

'Well. You'd. Better. Go. And. Get. It. Back. Right. NOW. '

My previously contented disposition dissipated as quickly as smoke rings and I was overcome with a sudden weakness:

'But…but…' tumbled from my mouth involuntarily, followed almost inaudibly by 'but I said he could have it.'

Implacably Mum retorted, 'well he can't have it. Go and get it back. NOW.'

And so, humiliatingly, tail between legs, I trudged off to Norman's house, tentatively pressed the doorbell and explained that regretfully I needed my horrible coat back, and that I was sorry.

I was occasionally sent to get emergency supplies from the local shops and am convinced that my speed was the inspiration for Amazon. I just couldn't resist running everywhere I went and would therefore sprint to whichever shop I was sent, money clasped firmly in hand. Focused entirely on whatever I needed to buy I then dashed out of the shop homewards with the 'prize', usually to be stopped in my tracks at the shop door by the friendly shopkeeper's exasperated voice: 'Don't forget your change.'

However, it was now time to earn some pocket money and I was designated two tasks. The first of these, the coal monitor, entailed me standing at the foot of the cellar steps whenever the coal man delivered. This was quite exciting as he dragged back the heavy metal lid, scraping on the concrete path, then an explosion of noise as the bags were tipped one after another down the hole, creating a 'mountain' of coal. Emerging through the plume of coal dust my job was to tidy up after the drop ensuring all the loose pieces of coal, nutty slack and dust were swept into a coherent shape, and the cellar was left clean and tidy. Not that there was anything in the cellar worth bothering about other than an abandoned old wringer, and Dad's homemade brew, which he never ever tasted, preferring to go to the Dog and Partridge of a night for a couple of pints.

My second assignment, official cleaner of the family shoes, turned out to be a labour of love. Cellar based, again, I effectively cleaned Dad's shoes and mine, as well as applying liberal amounts of dubbing to my football boots. In those far off days having well-polished shoes was de rigueur and Dad had often referred to his service days and the effectiveness of 'spit and polish'. I really applied myself to ensuring we had the shiniest shoes in the neighbourhood, using copious amounts of Kiwi Parade Gloss then spitting and polishing furiously until the dull wax slowly started to shine, then ultimately gleam. The shining of shoes was to my eyes a truly serious vocation: highly polished shoes being the mark of the man! Over time I honed my technique and, using a tip from one of my teachers, applied lashings of polish to the unlaced shoes, letting the polish soak into the leather overnight and then buffing them into submission the following day. This provided stupendous results with the bonus of leather preservation as well as a blinding gleam. I was so proud if, whenever our shoes went to the cobbler, he remarked on how well they'd been preserved.

I had a truly blessed childhood, playing my beloved soccer, running everywhere all the time, and with a bit of schooling thrown in. Never pressured, just allowed to be free. The happiest days of my life indeed.

Childhood Memories

PAUL HALLOWS

I had to go to Pendlebury Children's Hospital for an operation once.

To say thank you for their help my dad decided to do a sponsored swim for them.

My dad had cancer of the lung and the spine when I was born in 1979. The doctors gave him six weeks to live.

He was bedbound during this time. After a lot of help he managed to be free of cancer.

When he got his strength back he was in a wheelchair but could walk a short distance on walking sticks.

Anyway, to cut a long story short, he managed to do the sponsored swim. I was in the pool with him. I was only a child then and Dave Camm my swimming teacher was in the pool as well just to make sure my dad was ok.

My dad only planned to do two lengths but managed to do six.

His story ended up in the newspaper.

Primary School Scribbles

Aged 3-years, I was petrified; stuck on a platform at the top of the Nursery Class climbing frame which could not have been more than 5 feet high.

Allocated daily a small bottle of pasteurised milk to drink through a straw, invariably warm from being stored near a radiator. I loved it as we only had sterilised milk at home.

My eldest brother Gregory overhearing Mum & Dad muttering that my younger brother Michael had not received a nursery place, whereas a neighbour's only child two months younger had (her mother owned a hairdressing salon). Greg relayed this to his teacher the next day. Lo and behold Michael was promptly offered a place.

My Mum and Dad laughing when my third brother Stephen's teacher left as Miss Bashall for the summer break and returned at the autumn term as Mrs Box.

My Mum mortified when I returned from school with a drawing of my bedroom featuring a chamber pot under the bed. My Dad laughed and said so what, everybody had one.

My class of 7 years-old received the strap on both hands administered in anger when the culprit of a playground accident had run home. When indignantly telling of this after school, my Mum retorted: 'Well, you must have all deserved it.'

When collected by Mum from class to attend the school dentist and being told on the way that there was no H in aitch. Eh? Apparently not meant to be pronounced 'haitch'.

Being proud of creating rumpety-tumpety poetry only to realise that a bespectacled serious and studious girl in the class had produced pieces worthy of any Poet Laureate.

Enacting the moon when reciting Lewis Carroll's 'The Walrus & the Carpenter' held a hoop covered with yellow crepe paper through which I poked my head. A girl with as round a face as me was the sun with her head poked through an orange crepe paper hoop.

For a school show of Hans Christian Anderson's stories put to music, sulked when my Mum made me a costume to be one of eight marigolds because she had made a super outfit for a friend to be a furry creature. On the night of the Concert, my Mum was called out of the school hall to be told that her younger sister aged 31 years had died in childbirth and that we were to take my cousin Barry home with us.

My classmates cooingly talked of this cute-looking boy in nursery class named Desmond, sobbing throughout his first day at school. That was my youngest brother.

Once her brood was past infancy, Mum was accepted as a student teacher at my school (being the same one she had attended) but her weak heart meant she could not keep up with the rigours of everyday life – she hid her frustrations well but was yet another thwarted career-woman of her time. Anyway, who would make the clothes for our large extended family if otherwise occupied!

Junior Classes for boys were on a different school site. One of Greg's friends, aged 7 years, fresh to this new route as he returned after lunch, was fatally run over on a hump-backed bridge near my home.

Lustily singing 'The Skye boat song' on a Friday afternoon with the partitions pulled back so all junior classes could take part. Other favourites were sanitised versions from The National Song Book of 'Barbara Allen, 'Sweet Polly Oliver' and 'The Golden Vanity'.

As I progressed through primary school, at morning school assemblies, whenever we sang the hymn 'Lord for tomorrow and its needs I do not pray, set Thou a seal upon my lips just for today' I thought seal referred to a honking sea creature.

Whilst revising after school for 11-plus exam, informed of Manchester United Football Team air crash. Numbed with shock, recall running home through hushed streets.

More childhood memories

PAUL HALLOWS

The 80s, that was the era I grew up in. I lived in a bungalow with my mum and dad at the time. My dad was in a wheelchair after having a hard battle with lung and spine cancer. What a fighter he was! Given six weeks to live by the doctor in 1979 when I was born, he lived till 2007.

One of my earliest memories as a child was when I was about six or seven years old. I was given my first bike by my Uncle Bill. It was originally going to be given to another boy, the son of some friends of my uncles.

Anyway, to cut a long story short, the boy didn't want it as he said it was too old fashioned.

The lady asked my uncle, dad's brother who was one of seven, if he knew anyone who would appreciate it. So he suggested me.

When I was given the present I was over the moon and when I showed it to my mates, I was like the coolest kid ever. The bike was a Chopper. They are normally in red but mine was a special one - it was blue. I started off on stabilisers until I was ready to

have them taken off. I used to ride around the streets with my friends, sometimes having races.

Learning to ride helped me gain a badge in the scouts as well. The Cyclist Proficiency Badge. I had to learn all sorts of hand signals like turning left or right, slowing down and all sorts of things.

There was a lot to learn. I also learnt how to mend a puncture and lots of other useful skills.

Every year when I was in the cub scouts, aged eight to ten and a half years old, we used to enter into a carnival in Little Hulton and Walkden. There was a prize for the best float. We used to decorate a trailer of a truck with different themes every time.

One year we were Vikings in a long boat. We had to dress up as well. We had big oars that were stuck through holes at the side of the boat which were moveable so it looked like we were rowing the boat.

Another time we were Knights of the Round Table. We won that year. We won a shield which is still displayed in a cabinet at Worsley swimming baths with the name of our group, 3rd Worsley.

It was a really big event and the locals used to come out of their houses and wave at us. It was great fun.

Sylvia Edwards from Child to Teen

THE SIMPLICITY OF PLAY

My grandchildren, along with other kids today, cannot imagine life without phones, tablets and computers. But what wasn't there - wasn't missed. The fun lay outside when the weather allowed. Everyone in our street knew each other because we played out together.

Remember those long skipping ropes placed across the entire road? The older kids spun the rope for the younger ones. We played outside far more than children do today. But of course, we could because very few cars came up our street. If one did - it was likely to be the doctor or somebody socially 'higher up' than us. Any car parked on our street was a source of curiosity. We would peer through the windows, marvelling at this strange thing and wondering where the important person was going. Who was sick? What was the matter?

Some games haven't changed - tag, hide and seek, hopscotch and hula hoops, which my grandchildren still love. We also played leap frog- one child bent forwards, for the other to leap over him. The yoyo was also popular. We also had marbles, tiddlywinks and snakes and ladders. I remember juggling balls for hours against the walls of our house.

The films of the day also influenced play: as boys became

16

'Cowboys and Indians', running around and whooping. The lingering effects of war were also reflected in playful battles with pretend guns. I played a lot with my dolls; taking them for walks and lifting them in and out of their baby carriage. My dolls lay on beautiful bedding, just like a portable bed. I also had a lovely, pink rag doll that was soft and squidgy; like a cuddly friend in bed.

Our toys seemed simple compared with those of today. My dolls did not wee or cry. Cars were not remote. My brother pushed them along the floor and made appropriate noises. Pan lids and spoons did as drums. The games we played worked because we put our own sense of fun into them. Yet these simple things offered just as much pleasure as the most sophisticated tablets and devices now available for our latest generation. Children had to be inventive and creative. Did we, much of the time, invent our own fun? And did we learn to enjoy more - with less? I think we did.

CRAFTED WITH LOVE

World War Two was coming to an end as I emerged in the small town of Darwen, Lancashire. My memories start from about five years old. Most of my childhood seemed happy enough. My dad had come back from the war unharmed. How lucky I was: even though I did not realise it then.

Here is one of my first recollections. Imagine me, about five or six years old. It's dark. I lie in bed. Yet again, I have been wakened by the banging. But I am not frightened by this nightly noise. It's only Dad, pounding away in his workroom next door to the bedroom I share with my brother. The hammering goes on and on - then stops. Dad opens the door. His shadowy figure creeps around us. Does he smile? I like to think so. Then I hear the bedroom door close softly and his footsteps growing gradually fainter as he pads downstairs. I drift back to sleep.

I remember this because it was special. Weeks later, on Christmas morning, after yet more hammering and banging, the mystery was solved. A large parcel sat on the floor. I tore eagerly at the paper - to reveal a doll's house. How beautiful it was! The entire house was built of wood; each piece carefully crafted and shaped by Dad - even the tiny beds, table and chairs. My mother, bless her, had made some tiny curtains and bed covers. I was entranced by my tiny, fairylike house that was perfect in every detail.

I recall that special Christmas present because It had been made by someone I loved. I never wanted to give it away, even when, years later, I no longer played with it. That doll's house sat in my bedroom, taking pride of place, even amongst all the paraphernalia of my teens. Don't you think there is something special and comforting about toys that are homemade?

Dad also made my younger brother a fort, again out of wood, with soldiers. I remember this time as an era of war games - played with toy guns and swords.

How did we play in those distant days? I was brought up in a small terraced house, very working class, but I can't remember going without the things I needed. I say this because, so many years later, I can't believe how materialistic and commercial childhood has become, especially birthdays and Christmases. My grandchildren receive piles of presents that they open one after the other, the excitement seemingly in the pulling and tearing of wrapping paper, rather than in the joy of the gift itself. I wonder how they would react if there were one or two simple toys, along with an apple and an orange in a Christmas stocking. Imagine the shock!

GRAMMAR SCHOOL: 1956 -1961

Having passed the 11-Plus, I found myself amongst learners who took their learning, and their futures, very seriously. At Darwen Grammar School, I learned that education was the gateway to a good job but now look back and see both its flaws and its merits.

I remember sitting in mainly silent classrooms, often copying from the blackboard as teachers delivered lectures and gave us facts; to write down, make sense of - and remember. Learning was a one-way channel of communication. I don't remember being asked by any teacher about what I actually <u>thought</u> about the information received.

How times have changed. In modern classrooms, there is more talk, interaction and verbal communication between adults and learners, than there ever was during my school days. Children now are expected to offer their opinions, to challenge the facts they receive and to question 'why'. Today's learners have a voice!

If my grammar school peers and I had not been rational thinkers to some extent, would success have eluded us: given that the skills of challenge and interrogation seemed low on the school agenda? No doubt, we were expected to develop these skills ourselves.

Facts, facts, facts! Amongst those I memorised from school was that the Romans used Doric, Ionic and Corinthian columns to adorn public buildings. I recall little else about the Romans from those school days. Their qualities as a civilisation eluded me until later. But I remembered those columns because they were drilled into me, as forcefully as the dates of kings and queens, capital cities and the stages of volcanic eruption.

It seems strange now that we applied our maths to imperial money: of pounds, shillings and pence. Twelve pennies equalled one shilling and twenty shillings equalled one pound. Each penny was split into farthings and half pennies. Over a penny, we had threepenny bits, and the sixpence. Other coins were two shillings, known as florins, half-crowns (two shillings and sixpence), with eight to one pound, and crowns (five shillings), with four to one pound. There were also guineas worth twenty-one shillings. Imagine applying this complicated system if you were unlucky enough to have a specific numeracy difficulty (now labelled 'Dyscalculia'). Yet it all seemed natural to us (the UK 'went decimal' in 1971).

What did I hate? Hockey. I was terrified of being hit accidentally with these huge wooden sticks. One day, having got changed for PE, I hid in the changing rooms after the others had gone out to the field, hoping to avoid this torturous game. However, the teacher came back to get me. I was in trouble. I also hated the long cross-country runs up the big hill by the side of our school and across the fields at the back, then down again. I did not like getting slutchy and muddy and hated most team games, even netball.

Does this memory divulge anything about me as a team player? I recall myself as a timid young person - nervous and reluctant to join in organised games, or approach groups without first being invited. Was it because of possible failure? Would I let my team down if I threw the ball, then missed the net? Better to stay in the background? Definitely.

Which subjects did I like or dislike? I hated Science and did very badly. Even now I do not know the simplest things: how rain is formed or what happens when any chemicals are mixed together. But I loved languages (French and German) and English, in which I excelled. I also enjoyed Maths, maybe because the teacher who taught it also taught me to love the subject (in spite of never knowing why we learned algebra).

School then was gender-oriented. Girls learned needlework and cookery, while the boys did woodwork. I remember having to sew a cookery apron in the first year (now Year 7) and embroidering my name on. Sewing and craftwork have remained a feature of my life so maybe I was influenced by the cookery and sewing lessons at school.

Discipline was harsh, even outside the school gates. I remember getting in trouble for not wearing my school hat as I walked up the driveway. The hat was a horrible straw thing with a green ribbon around it, and I hated it. Then there was the cane. I never got it because I didn't dare say one word out of turn to any teacher. My brother went regularly to Mr Abbott's (headteacher) office to receive a number of hard whacks on the outstretched palm, with a length of bamboo. Imagine the outcry now! Child abuse, or what?

Who remembers their school hymn? Ours was Jerusalem. I can hear the echoes: our whole school singing this hymn in our huge assembly hall that had a balcony, and the teachers in their academic caps and gowns, on the stage.

I recall walking home from school in a group and buying 'penny dabs' from the chip shop. One time, I remember (with shame) us daring each other to steal something from the sweet shop. It was kept by an elderly lady who took ages to come through to serve from the back room. So we all stole a chocolate bar while we waited, shoved it into our blazer pockets, then bought another. I hope that old lady (now up there) has forgiven me.

Another (unpleasant) memory has ended up making me eternally grateful. I recall being pressured into trying a cigarette (probably behind the bike sheds). It was horrible! I coughed and spluttered and felt sick. That cigarette put me off smoking for life. How thankful I am that I tried it. In those days smoking was a cool thing to do and all the film stars did it. So I find it hard to understand, in this world of strong media warnings, how people continue to smoke.

Being at Grammar School was an interesting experience socially. I felt overawed in the company of children who came from 'higher up' the social scale. Not in the classroom, because I could hold my own in lessons, but at parties, for example. I remember being invited to a party at the house of someone who lived in a much more exclusive residence than my own and spending the entire time hanging around, afraid to join in. Was it me?

Was the '11-Plus' a good system or not? Divisive or opportunistic? Certainly, I was one of those children who, because of it, was enabled to climb the social ladder. But I'm sure that some of those who did not pass the 11-Plus, might easily have succeeded at Grammar if they had been given the chance to change track later on. The Tripartite system sorted children into three groups from age eleven - those suitable for Grammar, Technical or Secondary Modern schools. Children who 'failed' the 11-Plus attended either Technical or Secondary Modern. How unfair was it to attempt to channel children's futures by means of one exam? Ironically, the 11-Plus system is still with us in some areas of the country!

I was a late developer at Grammar. We had GCE's then (General Certificate of Education). My first form teacher wrote the following, as a summary of my varied percentage grades (22 Music, 29 Chemistry, 43 English, 69 Maths, 72 French): *'Sylvia must try very hard next term to improve on this performance. She should overcome her difficulties ....and not let them accumulate'.* My form position, at age 11, was 30th out of 34. One year later: '*A very good report, reflecting sound work. Sylvia is to be congratulated on her tremendous improvement.'* My form position was then 4th out of 28. Wow! Unfortunately, I dipped. Aged 15, I ended up with '*Good work has brought about good results in most subjects. Sylvia must, however, try harder in Maths'* (only 36%). Oh dear! It must have been the algebra! How ironic that I have ended up teaching it to GCSE!

In spite of my Grammar School education, and having achieved six GCE's, which at that time, were the gateway into A Levels, then University, I never experienced university life. My father got me a job with the Civil Service at age sixteen. I don't recall any conversations with my parents about my future. I left school, was allowed two weeks of the summer holiday, then started work as a Clerical Assistant at the Telephone Manager's Office: all arranged by my father. Was this because our family was short of money, or was it because I was working class, and university was not something that our family had ever thought about? Both, I suppose. My brother never went to university either. I never remember being pushed by my parents to make the best of myself - only later, as a mature student, (aged 27) did I push myself to where I wanted to be.

A COUNTRY GIRL: 1956 TO 1963

Why is it that I am 'in my element' striding happily across open moors with the wind tugging at my hair? It has to be my country upbringing. Ken Robinson first coined this phrase in a book *Finding Your Element*: our 'element' being something we do that feels completely natural to us and that resonates strongly within us. My element is being out in the open, on my own, with nothing but nature surrounding me. Also my name happens to mean wood nymph.

I must have been about eleven when my family moved from a terraced house in Darwen to a dilapidated farm on Bull Hill, a huge area of moorland between the town and Bolton. The farmhouse needed a lot of doing up. It even had a septic tank. My dad seemed to spend years doing up this place and it was never finished. I recall regularly having to break the ice on top of the horse trough at the front of the farmhouse to get water for drinking and washing. No running water! Looking back - it seemed as if 'doing up' properties was my dad's passion. What a pity he wasn't better at it. He might have become a nineteen fifties property developer. As it was, we would have been warmer and more comfortable living in a post-war prefab!

Getting to school was no easy matter. First there was the two mile walk along the farm track to the road, followed by a half mile down to the bus stop. Darwen Grammar was about two miles from there into the town centre, then a further three miles from the centre along Blackburn Road. I soon got used to it.

Our farm was too far away for me to have birthday parties or friends to visit. But somehow I didn't mind. I suppose I got used to being alone. There was so much wildlife to entertain me - rabbits playing on the grass or birds pecking around. The silence was golden!

Our family circumstances took a turn for the worse when my dad had an accident with a tractor and broke his leg badly. He then ceased farming and set up his own night-time security business. We still lived on the farm but without animals. A little later, my mother managed an off-licence in the town so sometimes, instead of going directly up to the farm, I walked from school to the off-licence, then waited until it closed at nine o'clock for my father to collect us and take us home.

Then began an association with guard dogs. My dad's security business meant that he had a few Alsatians, housed in the barn at the side of the farmhouse, which he took with him every night to the factories he protected. Heaven help any potential burglar who might have come against my dad's dogs. They were fearsome creatures. I did not dare venture into the barn or even go outside when they were roaming.

My teenage years were spent on this hill top farm so my social life was curtailed. However, when I started to go dancing at St. George's hall in Blackburn, I walked the two miles or so down our farm track, stuck my walking shoes into a hole in the stone wall, changed into my dancing shoes, walked down to the Cemetery where the bus came up, then turned around, caught it into Darwen Centre, then caught a second bus into Blackburn.

If I was lucky, the return journey was sometimes different. When I got off the bus from Blackburn, there would often be a policeman on late evening patrol. I knew some of the police because my dad liaised with them through his security business. So I regularly got a lift in a police car up to Bull Hill, where I would collect my walking shoes from the hole in the wall and walk back up to our farm.

Walking home across wild moorland, after midnight, at the end of a Saturday night out, may have been an inconvenience - but was not so awful. I had been brought up to love walking amongst hills and the emptiness was never frightening. It was a little spooky because the outer wall of our local cemetery was just down the hill to my right. Noises in the night could be unnerving!

I don't recall 'stranger danger' being much of an issue, although my grandmother insisted I carry a pot of pepperr when I went out at night. What I would have done with it if attacked, I don't know. I can only imagine how useful it might have been if a sex maniac had sneaked up behind me on my walks. No female other than Superwoman (if she had been around then) would have been able to yank the thing out of her bag or pocket, get her hand free, then shake the pepper accurately into an assailant's eyes. It would have been better to kick the guy in his balls (but I knew nothing about such things then - did I?).

I remember learning to dance with my friend, Maureen. We went on Saturday mornings to learn traditional ballroom - waltz, foxtrot, tango, quickstep - as well as Latin American, including the Jive. We had tests for each dance, awarded by the United Kingdom Alliance of Professional Teachers of Dancing - I often got highly commended; being quite good at dancing, and if I may say so, I had good rhythm and style.

Those dance lessons taught me how to respond to the rhythm of any music. I always felt that dancing was a basic social skill for young ladies - at a time when dance halls were the main social venues.

At sixteen, we still lived on the farm. My first boyfriend had an aunt at Birkenhead, so I remember sailing across the Mersey on one of the newly-built commuter ferries; an interesting experience. This friend took me to the Cavern Club, though not to see the Beatles - how magical that would have been! Like most of my peers, I was a big Beatles fan. By 1962, the Cavern Club had become one of the most exciting pop venues in the world - where the Beatles made their name, also featuring other sixties groups such as Gerry and the Pacemakers, Billy J Kramer, the Searchers and The Fourmost. What an atmosphere! The Cavern, built in the French style of a cave, exploded during the early sixties. It was anything but comfortable, being hot and crowded with its domed ceiling and brick-styled walls. But the atmosphere carried it! Was I one of those screaming, demented girls? Definitely!

My parents never seemed to bother where I went or who with. Having stayed the night with my boyfriend's Aunt, the following day would see me back on the farm track - with the freedom of the open air, striding between grass and sky with nothing man-made in sight, probably humming a Beatles song.

Happy teenage days!

Much Ado About Nothing.

ALAN RICK

My school, an all-boy's school, taught us much about creation. We listened in real or feigned rapture, as the black-gowned master explained how a variety of things came into existence: how the frog developed from the tadpole, how the plants and flowers arose from seeds, how the butterfly emerges from the chrysalis and many wonders by which nature manifested herself. Several years later, in the army, an irate drill sergeant was to express wonder that I had managed to make it to the human race at all and to cast doubt on my parentage by calling me a 'clueless b.......!' But for the present, all seemed to be in order. Yet one question remained to be answered: how did I get here? Apparently, I was one of the many creations by which the Lord moved in mysterious ways, His wonders to perform. It would have astonished the drill sergeant to hear that the Lord had even fashioned me as fit for military service – irony indeed.

The Headmaster had announced, in a voice that would have blown a hole in a wall, that the First Form were to receive a lesson in what was known as the 'human reproductive system.' Nobody in our form, twelve years old, had the remotest idea what it meant, but discussion in the quad threw up some exciting ideas. Those with a scientific leaning suggested that it must be about producing people by machine, an idea culled from the space adventure films becoming popular at the time. The old 'birds and the bees' theory we roundly dismissed as being fit only for infant school tots. We twelve-year old sophisticates were not to be palmed off with such stuff. Also, the stork cannot have brought us here – it was a long flight from Australia and we had never heard of his burden being lost by accident or by the sea. None of our parents had a gooseberry bush in their garden either. There was a quiet murmur from a be-spectacled boy in the front of the group that if you went to sit on a chair upon which a girl had already sat, a baby would be born due to the warmth of the seat she had sat on. This was greeted with scorn – no girl in our former primary school was capable of sitting long enough for this to happen. In any case, this was heresy – reproduction by purely human agency so clearly contrary to the thirty-nine articles of the Church of England. We knew this through our instruction in R. I. lessons.

Enter Hamilton, the Aristotle of our form, who was reputed to have the answer to everything in life, 'You lot are way off the track,' and we were sure he would have a theory. Whenever Hamilton adopted a lofty tone it always meant that he was having a theory.

'Your parents get together,' he answered mysteriously. But our parents are already together, was our reply, so clarification was required. 'Yes, but they do things to each other.'

There were blank stares all round as the mystery deepened.

'What things?'

'Well, things they don't tell anybody about.'

The stares got bleaker.

'Did my parents do this?' was my plaintive cry.

'They certainly did.'

I was seized with panic. 'Do the police know? Will they be prosecuted?'

'Not to worry,' answered our form lawyer. 'It's not a crime under the Official Secrets Act, but only a misdemeanour and the police have decided to let it go.'

In due course our visiting tutor, himself a wonder of creation, a fresh-faced, spindly youth full of the burning ardour of those determined to propel any novelty into the modern world, appeared. Our school was founded in the 15th century and, we thought, our masters not long after it, so it occurred to us that it would take an almighty heave to bring it into the 20th century. But we were attentive while he explained the process to us.

It seems that it was all about ducks, a figure of speech as we later realised to our relief.

'Have you noticed as you stroll through St James's Park how the ducks interact on the lake?' This was stirring stuff indeed. 'It is the male duck that makes the strident quacking noise to please the female.'

It was a wonder to us that she could be so easily pleased. The enlightenment went on from one absurdity to the next with the result that we all ended up no wiser than at the start. The picture of my father, a military man of stern character, making quacking noises to my mother was too surreal to be true. His noise would be much more earth-shaking than that. In time of war he was a man of peace – except in his domestic affairs.

The time for our post-lesson discussion in the quad at last arrived. Hamilton assumed his usual managerial air.

'We are getting another lesson next week,' he announced.

A voice from the back row murmured.

'Not those bloody ducks again!'

60s child in Switzerland and Italy

VERONICA SCOTTON

The town in Italy where Paolo was born in 1957, comprised of 3 villages. Merlo, Fabbri, and Mocellini. Surrounded by mountains the families rarely travelled out of the area and so 90% of the population were named Campana, (from Merlo) Mocellin (from Mocellini) or Scotton (from Fabbri)

When his parents married in April 1956, his mum moved in with her in-laws and took over the care of them. She was surprised that they hardly grew any food as her family grew everything. She started a vegetable garden and so by the time Paolo was born a year later, she could put fresh vegetables on the table every day. Along the bottom of their garden ran the River Brenta so during the fishing season they ate a lot of fish, they also kept chickens and rabbits for the table. Tecla's brother had a job as a game warden for a land owner and would occasionally bring along a pheasant to supplement their diet.

There was hardly any industry around and most people were poor farmers, the house in which they lived had been in the family for 3 generations and very neglected, but she could see the potential, if they only had the money to do the repairs.

Around this time, Giovanni (Gildo) Paolo's dad joined a group of builders recruited to build a school in St Maurice in Switzerland. He could only get a level A Visa which meant that he could only work for nine months each year, and then he would return home and work on the farm or find part time building work.

In 1957 Gildo joined a crew of builders building a large house high up in the Italian Alps. Normally getting a lift up the mountain on Monday, working all week and then returning home on Friday for the weekend. On the last weekend in March he had been persuaded by the lure of overtime rates to work the weekend. On Monday 1st April, his brother drove up the mountain to tell him that Tecla had given birth to a son, he had become a father for the first time. Tecla had had a bad time and was being treated in hospital, he needed to go home. Gildo was not gullible and at first refused to stop work. 'It's 1st April and I'm no fool' he answered. However eventually he was persuaded but all the way down the mountain threatened his brother that if this was a prank he would have to pay his lost wages. They drove straight to the hospital where he met his firstborn, Paolo a beautiful blue eyed, blond son.

Eventually Tecla recovered from the birth and planned to apply for a Swiss Visa so that she could spend more time with her husband, but her mother-in-law persuaded her to stay, promising her that if she stayed to look after them until they died, they would leave the house and land to Gildo.

A year later, they died within 6 months of each other and they discovered that the promise of the house was a cruel ploy. The house had been used as collateral for years to raise dowries for their daughters and buy farming equipment for their sons. The debt they had inherited far outstripped what the house was worth.

Tecla finally got her visa, unbelievably a class B which meant she didn't have to return to Italy every 9 months, and the little family moved into a small house with another family. They had one bedroom, Paolo had to share a bed with his parents and they shared a kitchen with the other family, two brothers and sister. One of the brothers was a priest and the other two siblings were very religious. Within a year they found a more suitable place to live. It was rooms in another building, they had two bedrooms and their own kitchen and bathroom. Another family in the building were an Italian family, Signori Simoncini. Tecla paid them to look after Paolo and she got a job cooking for the priests in the Basilica nearby.

Paolo has a memory of this family locking their son in a coal cellar for misbehaving. He learned at a very young age to be fearful of these childminders and didn't give them an opportunity to lock him in there. This family moved out a year later and a Swiss Family Madame and Monsieur Dirac moved in. They took over as Paolo's carers. Tecla was working more and more for the priests, washing and ironing, making beds, cleaning dormitories in the student accommodation. When they moved for the third time to a three bedroom apartment, Paolo stayed with the Swiss family whom he loved. His parents decided that he would be better off with them, he would learn to speak fluent French before starting school. Paolo's language skills soon outstripped his parent's and he has a memory of going home one weekend and being unable to understand their Italian dialect. Monsieur Dirac was a carpenter and had a workshop on the ground floor of the building, he let Paolo 'help' by sweeping up the sawdust etc. He showed him how to use his hand tools but barred him from the workshop when using the rotary saw or other electrical equipment. At the time the carpenter was mostly employed to build furniture, years later his skills were used to build coffins. In the building next door to the workshop, was the milking shed for the local dairy farmer, Paolo helped him to herd the cows in for milking and was rewarded with a glass of warm milk, straight from the cow, he still thinks back nostalgically to this time.

In 1962, aged 5, Paolo was enrolled into the reception class of Ecole de Primaire de St Maurice the school his dad had helped to build a few years before. Tecla took a week off from work to take him to school, embarrassingly on his first day as his mum chatted to another parent, a teacher came out into the playground and told all the young children to give their mum a kiss and to get into line. Embarrassingly, Paolo turned around and kissed the lady standing behind him only to discover it was not his mum.

The school to this day looks very modern. All the pupils had to change into black gym shoes before entering the classroom, the reception children also had to wear an apron. The reception class was taught by a Nun from the local convent and she changed his name to Paul (this would be surely classed as racism today) and this was the name he used for the rest of his school years. Girls and boys had separate entrances, the girls classrooms and playground on a higher level, Paolo remembers the boys standing trying to catch a glimpse of the girls knickers from their lower vantage point. During this time Paolo still lived with the Swiss family. They had three children, each of them older than him, Jacqueline, Jean Michel and George Albert. From the second week onwards, George took him to school, he helped him with his homework and he became his God Father or sponsor when he was confirmed. Every year there was a gymnastic tournament in Canton Valais and all the schools competed there, Paolo stayed later at school two afternoons a week to train for this, and George Albert would bring him home later in the evening.

At the weekends while Paolo was at home with his parents, they sometimes invited friends home for a meal. Their son Eric came with them and while the adults gossiped, Eric and Paolo played football in the courtyard, using an old dead tree as a goalpost. He badgered Paolo to say which was his favourite football team. Paolo was not particularly interested in football but on a whim said Inter Milan. He still supports them to this day. Tecla's cookery skills became well known and often one or other priest would invite himself in for Sunday dinner, always followed by a glass or two of Grappa.

During the first year of school, the children were not introduced to writing at all. They did drawing and colouring and playing. In the next year when writing was introduced they did not use pencils but from the beginning pen and ink, very messy in the hands of 6 year old children. The school was open from Monday to Saturday, with a lunchtime finish on Wednesday and Saturday. On Wednesday afternoon, Paolo attended Italian school where he learned to speak proper Italian, not the dialect spoken by his parents and the geography and history of Italy. One weekend he mithered his parents asking 'Am I allowed to get an apple from school?' They answered him puzzled, 'Of course you can, why do you need to ask?' The next day he came home with a receipt. He should have asked 'Am I allowed to buy an apple from school?' They were incensed, they had apple trees growing in the allotment and money was so tight, they really didn't need to be buying apples.

Each year on Assumption Thursday the children had a parade around town dressed as a Saint. One year Paolo was dressed as St Paul complete with a long white robe, and a halo fashioned from a tinsel covered, wire coat hanger. Behind him was a boy called Maurice dressed as St Joseph. He carried a hammer and repeatedly hit Paolo on the head with it, in time to the walking band, until he

32

was spotted by an adult and the hammer confiscated.

By the time Paolo was about 7 his mum was becoming increasingly irritated because the priests continued to expect more work from her, but never increased her wages. Speaking to them one Sunday after they had their fill of good food and Grappa she brought up the subject of a wage increase and was angry to receive the reply that she should not ask for wages when doing God's work. The next time a priest called she told them that her wages did not run to buying Grappa, they found another catholic woman to provide their Sunday Dinner and she stopped attending Sunday Mass. The rift became wider and when she became pregnant with her second child, she left the employ of the church and began working from home, cutting small metal parts for use by watch makers. She was contracted to cut 10,000 pieces a day, which initially took 6 hours. She had a few different machines that she used for individual parts. One of them was quite noisy, which annoyed the neighbours, another was slightly quieter but was very tiring as she had to pull down a lever 10,000 times. Paolo used to ride his mum's bike to return the cut pieces and pick up more raw materials. He had to wait while a sample of the pieces was checked out, if they weren't precise enough an engineer would be dispatched to her house to adjust the machine. Alongside of this she still did 90% of all the housework, Cleaning, cooking, sewing and knitting clothes for the family and preserving the produce from the garden to last them through winter. She decided that she could not continue to pay for Paolo to live with the Dirac's and he sadly left the family he loved. On 17th March 1965 Pietro was born and Paolo was put into service looking after his brother. He was never allowed to play out unless he took Pietro with him. At the tender age of 8 years he learned to change a nappy. Following his first communion, Paolo became an altar boy but stopped serving on the altar when he was told that the priests used the collection money to visit the prostitutes in the next town.

One of his other chores at this time was being sent to the allotment each morning before school. His parents had acquired this plot of land during their first year in Switzerland and used it to grow fruit, vegetables and herbs and also to keep chickens and rabbits. Each day Paolo was sent there to feed the chickens, collect the eggs and also to bring back any vegetable that his mum needed to cook the dinner. At first he walked but then as soon as his legs were long enough he was allowed to ride his mum's or dad's bike.

Every Tuesday at school, a priest from the local church came to lecture them. One week, Paolo had forgotten to bring in his catechism book and the priest sent him home to get it. He ran home and sneaked into the house to retrieve it, hoping that his mum would not find out. But unfortunately for him, Monsieur Cure knew his mum well and soon informed her of her son's misdemeanour. When he returned home from school she banned him from watching TV or playing out on the bike for a month. He wasn't bothered about the TV but very disappointed about not being able to ride the bike. The bike was not his, he never had one of his own until he was old enough to buy one for himself, it was his mum's. She didn't think about this until she wanted him to take her weekly delivery to the watch making factory. Paolo reminded her that it was too far for him to walk and so the bike ban was dropped. On one of these trips, the rain was pouring down, he was riding too fast and didn't see a car rounding the corner until he collided with it. He was thrown through the air, over the top of the car to land on the opposite side. With the flexibility of youth he escaped with hardly a scratch, unfortunately his mum's bike was flattened. She was not best pleased

On the other hand, while larking in the snow one winter on the way to school, he slipped and dislocated his collar bone. When the chance came for him to go on a skiing trip with the school, his dad said 'you can't even walk to school safely, you are definitely not safe to slide down a mountain' . Years later as an adult, he had an opportunity to experience skiing and never mastered the art of stopping, so perhaps his dad had a point.

At the end of each school year in June, each teacher would organise a trip for the pupils. Paolo remembers going by train and coach to Mont Blanc, Les Marecotte Mountain Zoo, and Zermatt ski resort from where they could see the Matterhorn. One year they travelled to Fribourg to visit the gruyere cheese making factory and another time to the chocolate factory. Each year on return from these trips they were met at the station by the town band who would lead them dancing and singing back to the school yard as a celebration to mark the beginning of their long school summer break.

In year six, a rota was made for the children to act as school crossing patrol (no lollipop ladies there). Two kids each day at 11.30 and 4.30 with a signal paddle in each hand would stop the traffic while the rest of the school children safely crossed each of the two main roads.

Paolo did not lose touch with the family that had brought him up for 6 years. He would visit them at the weekend and also go to see them on occasions when he needed help with homework. Tecla took more of an interest in her eldest son at this time, especially when he showed an interest in cooking. Soon he had learned to pluck a chicken and skin a rabbit although to this day has never actually killed the animal. He can remember at the age of 10 cooking a full Sunday dinner without help. He learned to knit and make himself a scarf, which turned out very long because he could not master casting off.

Every Sunday after church, dressed in their Sunday Best the family joined their Italian neighbours in the Community centre. The children played together, mindful not to get their Sunday best clothes dirty, the women gossip and drink coffee, the men gossip and drink coffee and grappa. At Christmas, parties were organised for the 6th January, the Epiphany when traditionally gifts are exchanged in Italy. Each child had to 'do a party piece' either sing or tell a joke or poem. At Easter the women baked traditional Easter cakes and throughout the rest of the year there were organised barbecues and dances. At that time there were more Italians than Swiss people living in St Maurice, but they were still referred to as 'the foreigners' many Swiss people still do refer to them this way and blame them for everything they feel wrong with the town, despite the fact that most of the town was built using Italian labour.

The summer holidays from school lasted for 10 weeks. Each year the family caught the train for the eight hour journey to Italy, where they made repairs and improvements on the house. Gildo would stay for 2 weeks while Tecla and the boys stayed longer.

Paolo's Paternal Grandparents

After the grandparents died the rest of the Scotton family neglected the farm to some extent. Using the land only for growing tobacco and grapes. One year Paolo was given the task of picking the tobacco leaves and then using a large needle and thread to fasten them together, hang them up to dry. He accidentally speared himself with the needle and began to cry at the sight of the blood, he is still squeamish, his older cousins made fun of him for being soft. I imagine that he was a very gentle boy and he received a lot of teasing from his uncles and cousins who wanted to toughen him up. The farm had lots of rabbits running around free which would be caught to eat whenever needed, there were also a number of feral cats. Paolo had one cat that he regarded as a pet, it would sleep on his bed each night he stayed there. One day as he was enjoying a meal with his granddad and cousin Andrea, they asked him whether he was enjoying the meal, he answered yes it was delicious. They asked 'and how's the rabbit meat' once again he answered that it was very nice, he wondered why they were exchanging grins. It turned out that the meat he was enjoying was his pet cat. He refused to eat rabbit at the farm after that, although in hindsight admits that it tasted very good. God knows how he has turned out to the kind and gentle man he is.

One of his jobs during these holidays was to get up at 6 am to walk up the mountain to his maternal grandparent's house to collect some milk from the goat and sometimes bring back home made salami. While there, he would feed the chickens and donkey and then have a ride on it. One day he got on the donkey and kicked his heels to make it walk, instead he was tossed over the donkey's head into the mud. His granddad saw it and said, 'Well you'll not forget to feed him first, next time'.

One day he was persuaded to take his little brother with him for the walk. He decided to take a different route and became lost at one point, having to balance along a narrow ledge with a long drop below them. Pietro didn't stop crying and never came with him again.

From the age of 10 he joined the school camp which was held in the mountains for the first two weeks of the school summer break. At home they always ate homemade bread and jam for breakfast, but on camp they had musli, which he hated and dawdled over. But he found out that the last child to finish had to wash the dishes. After three days of washing 40 breakfast dishes, he learned to eat quicker whether he liked it or not. The boys and girls on camp slept in separate dormitories but shared a lot of the activities during the day. They learned to throw knives at a target, whittle wood into toys and even to sew and knit. They had a lot of free time, being summoned from their play for meals by a bell. One day Paolo and 3 more boys went exploring the woods and got lost, wandering further and further away as they tried to find their way back to camp. Only when they didn't turn up when the bell rang at 4 pm did the leaders realise they were missing. A search party was sent and the errant boys found later in the evening. Whenever the camp leaders could find fault, they would use the culprits to do the jobs needed on camp and so these four were on dormitory cleaning duty for the rest of the week. He was easily led and was persuaded on one occasion to trickle water from a jug into a bucket in earshot of a boy who had on occasion wet the bed. It had the desired effect of inducing more wet sheets. The poor boy had to wash and dry his bedding, but they did not escape punishment. They couldn't help but boast about the prank and when news got back they were on the shopping detail. They had to walk for two miles to the nearest shop to buy bread and milk and to post and collect the letters from the post office. All the children were instructed to write a letter home each day, telling their parents what they had been doing.

At the middle weekend of the camp, Paolo's parents and little brother walked the 3 miles up the mountain to visit him, bringing food and drink for a picnic, before walking back down again.

Around about this time, Tecla's younger brother Marino came to live with them for a couple of years to look for work. He would persuade the gullible Paolo to prank his brother and parents and then sit back and watch the sparks fly. Paolo to this day doesn't know why he thought he wouldn't get into trouble for pissing in his dads work boots or putting stinging nettles in their bed, or tying shoe laces together from under the table, while friends were getting drunk on grappa.

The first Christmas after Marino came to live with them, a magical thing happened, Father Christmas on a sleigh pulled by a donkey came to the house to deliver presents. Paolo, still desperate to believe in Santa pushed to the back of his mind that this one reminded him very much of his uncle. Pietro was enthralled!

When Paolo was 13 his elders began to question him about what he wanted to be after he left school. His first choice was to become a priest. They could hardly stop laughing and didn't take this choice seriously. He toyed with the idea of being a hairdresser which also was ridiculed, but when he said he wouldn't mind working in a restaurant, that seemed acceptable. Madam Dirac had a friend with a restaurant at the top of a mountain and suggested he got some work experience. So for the next three years he didn't join the family holiday to Italy, nor go to school camp, he went to live in the restaurant and worked there for 10 weeks. In the beginning his main job was to sweep the terrace and lay the tables, this also occasionally entailed rushing out to bring in the table cloths if it started raining and re-laying them when it stopped. Today it would be classed as child exploitation, but Paolo loved it and learned many of the skills needed to run a restaurant.

The restaurant was part of a ski resort and so relatively quiet in July and August unless they got a coach party. On coach party days he would work very long hours but on the other days he had a few hours in the middle of the day to lounge in his room or walk in the mountains. One day he set out to walk to the top of a particular mountain, intending to ride the cable car back down again. When he got to the top it was so cloudy that there was no view to see and it was beginning to thunder. He quickly boarded the cable car, unfortunately not noticed by the attendant. Half way down the car stopped. It wasn't used during storms. Paolo suspended in the middle was terrified for his life as he was tossed and thrown about clinging to the hand rails as he was sure that the doors would fly open and he would fall to his death. A couple of hours later as the storm subsided the cable car returned to full service and the attendant was shocked when this young trembling boy with a tear streaked face, staggered out. He was of course late for work by then and had his meagre wages docked.

Back at school, he began to neglect his work. Why should he bother when he knew he would have a job to go to? But at that time, if you didn't pass end of year exams, then you weren't allowed to graduate to the next class. Paolo, already one of the tallest in the class felt stupid the following year towering over his classmates who were a year younger. At the end of the following year with dire warnings from his parents he tried his best to get good marks. Just as he had finished, another pupil thought it would be good fun to 'accidentally' knock over the ink pot which obliterated his work. Paolo was so upset that he pushed the boy who, caught unaware, fell backwards and was knocked out. That was the first and last time that he has ever hit out in anger. The school did not make allowances for the loss of the work, nor give him the opportunity to resit the exam, he just had to stay behind another year.

Did my infancy succeed another age of mine that dies
before it? Was it that which I spent within my mother's
womb? And what before that life again, O God of my joy,
was I anywhere or in any body?

Confessions of St. Augustine....

Beyond the Womb

ROSEMARY SWIFT

Mid-May 1947. My heavily pregnant Manchester Mum is
wandering the gardens of a Cottage Hospital in Prestbury,
Cheshire; her local Maternity Hospital having been bombed during
WW2 and still not fully operational. Any troublesome pregnancies
such as hers have been farmed out. Rhodendrons are in full bloom
and it inspires her to choose the name, if she is carrying a girl, of
Rosemary. That is me in the womb: 'rosemary for sweet
remembrance' Shakespeare recorded. It will come to pass that I
will be interested in the arts - with not a scientific bone in my
body. I am three weeks overdue and have caused my Mum to swell
alarmingly. She has an infant son and will go on to have three
more sons but I her only daughter am causing her anxiety. My
Dad's preference is for a clutch of little girls so he will be thrilled
when I am born; also because I will be a fellow Cestrian, he being
Stockport born. My Mum is being closely monitored as she has
valvular heart disease, which - although cherished by a loving
husband - will claim her life at the age of 51 years. My own health
problems will mirror hers to some degree; also I am beginning to
deteriorate in the womb and will suffer from severe eczema. Later
this evening, I will be forced to be born and the Irish Midwife will
declare that I have eyes like 'violet pools'. Alas, my eyes are
infected and my finger and toe nails are septic. Health blips will
not hold me back in life – I will have jobs I enjoy, a lifelong
support network of family and friends, a loving husband and much
wanted children and adored grandchildren.

Snoozing...yawning...stretching...lulled along on a gentle rollercoaster ride, visually aware of serene blues, soothing greens and mellow yellows, I am disinclined to make my presence felt - not wanting to be thrust into an existence outlined for me... surrounding shadows with hushed voices, seemingly connected to past matriarchs, relay wishes that I fulfil hopes and dreams and aspirations of their own past earthly existences - to make sense of daily struggles and alleviate the harrowing loss of their own infants...

After a period of recuperation, my Mum will bring me home to Manchester during a heat wave. In her early stage of pregnancy, I am in the womb throughout one of the coldest winters ever recorded. Is this why I will have an aversion to extreme climates? I suspect I was conceived in The Orkneys where my Dad, Mum and elder brother had spent a holiday; my Dad keeping a promise to return, having been stationed there during WW2 with his Regiment, the Gordon Highlanders. When eventually sent to Europe, he was given the usual injections on a troopship – as they did not take, he was re-injected in the nipples. I also will not 'take' when given infant inoculations and will be re-injected on the soles of my feet.

In my inner city area, I will be educated by nuns and will diligently attend Mass and Communion and Confession and Benediction. Also, not to be missed will be the Saturday cinema matinee, the weekly comics and regular trips to the Library. My family will be voracious readers, in my case coming in handy when spending time in bed recovering from repeated bouts of tonsillitis. Many other hours will be spent playing in the streets; one seasonal activity is that of collecting bonfire wood from bombed houses. All the more reason to make a trip to the Municipal Baths, having outgrown the tin bath in front of the kitchen range on a Saturday evening, where after my hair will be put in rags to produce ringlets for Sunday, my hair in pigtails for the remainder of the week. Alas, for my Mum who will sew, knit and embroider for all of her extended family – especially Whit Week attire - I will be a tomboy, coming home from the Red Rec with frocks torn at the waist and missing hair ribbons. Dainty girl cousins will visit my maternal grandparents next door and play out with me without so much as gaining a smudge on their faces. I am never to be the demure lady my Mum wishes for from her only daughter, despite my birth offering up such a dream.

Dark spectres chase me... I run to the shelter of paler spirits... a primeval force pushes me down the birth canal and I am confused... demons battle: do I or not succumb to pressure to vacate the safe haven of this womb... voices urge: come, we will take your spirit to a new dimension... could an earthly demise mean joining active life-force within the galaxy or would I languish in limbo in nether regions should the universe not welcome my passivity...

A house move to the suburbs is an improvement in family circumstances as by now we number seven. (A decade or so earlier my Dad is amused by a Northumberland soldier relaying that he has four loons and a quine, which curiously transpires to be that of his own offspring of four boys and a girl.) There are gardens front, rear and side, an upstairs bathroom and a hall telephone. Morning mists muffle the crying of caged peacocks in the adjacent Park, which has impressive flower beds and where tennis can be played for four pennies and sizeable crowds watch the weekly football matches - especially pitchside of the local, very successful, ladies' team, whose medals, plaques and cups are displayed in the local chip shop window.

However, having passed the 11-plus examination just months before entails me travelling the length and breadth of Manchester to the High School, also turning out on Saturdays to play netball for the school team, so it is not too surprising that in Third Year I succumb to a family weakness by contracting rheumatic fever. When told I will miss school for at least six weeks, I cry my eyes out. It transpires that, following complications with my recovery, I will miss a whole school year and end up, after a brief period at the local secondary school, attending a two-year intensive secretarial course.

As a teenager in the 60s, with money jangling in my pockets from my first job, I frequent the abundant trendy Coffee Bars (garbed beatnik style in sloppy joe jumpers, long skirts and plaid stockings), progressing to preen at the fashionable Variety Clubs (adorned in low cut dresses, silk stockings and stiletto heels). Following on from the austere 50s, there is a buzz in the English air and a prevailing sense that anything can be achieved. Despite toying with the idea of working abroad, I do what is still ingrained in girls of my generation - I marry young, thus entering into many decades of life in Salford; becoming part of its fabric. My Anglo Saxon (with some Scottish roots) husband is stalwart and resolute, practical and determined. I being a mix of mostly Irish, some English, and a trace of Welsh, will always have a dreamy Celtic soul and will be vulnerable in early adult years to the winsome ways of others.

Shrouded in swirling cosmic matter, pulsating siren music lures me to embrace the maelstrom of whirling planetary forces... wearied, I innately know it is my destiny to join the earthly fight and once recognised the fluttering images of my future are fading, fading, fading...

For all my flaws, I will try to lead a decent and useful life – a decision lying within the soul of each and every human being; in the dark corners of my cognitive memory I sense our ultimate destiny will be to form matter (be it pure or evil in its nature) in the ether. Troughs of despondency will follow periods of loss, anxiety and angst, seemingly more frequent than the times of high elation and excitement. Traumas will serve only to strengthen my resolve to emerge unscathed into a well-balanced individual. For the most part, I will have a very ordinary and mundane life following a traumatic and frantic birth. By earthly standards, being born mid 20th century into the Western hemisphere will ensure I never suffer famine, dire poverty, or war on my own doorstep. Albeit stemming from a working class background of pulling oneself up by one's bootstraps, as a female I will always have options in the workforce. I will not be trapped like women of past generations into an existence of vapours brought on by frustration and damning of ambition enforced by the male of the species.

In turmoil and distress, I am forced to make my fevered entry onto the earthly plain... I cannot now pull back into the universal turbulence... as I am propelled into the light any remaining snapshots of my projected earthly existence evaporate... beyond the womb via the birthing bed there is just an urgent mewling and primeval need for the teat..

Judith Barrie - Happy Days

I have no recollection of my earliest toys, but there are a couple of photographs of me as a baby holding various playthings. There is a soft toy looking like a puppy or kitten – difficult to tell, but the expression on my face gives the impression that I wasn't too enamoured by it. There is a picture with a rubber duck and one with an ebony elephant, which I do recall. It was a present from my Uncle Jack, who was in the merchant navy after the war and brought all manner of exotic gifts from his travels to the 'Gold Coast', most of which ended up on the mantelpiece.

There is also a photo of a scruffy toddler with a dirty face, un-posed for once, intent on the teaspoon I was carrying, which, if I remember correctly, was full of soil. I had decided it needed to be taken from the front garden to fill in a hole in the back. A trait I retained all my life, of doing things the hard way!

On visits to my grandmother in Salford I was never a crumb of trouble. She had an ancient out-of-tune piano in the front parlour – never used except for very special occasions – and I was lifted onto the piano seat and allowed to 'play', usually singing some little ditty to accompany the playing. This would keep me amused for hours while the grown-ups talked in the kitchen round the fire. If I did get fed up, she had a wondrous tin full of buttons to root through, where I would find 'jewels': odd bits of broken brooches and necklaces and she often let me take some of them home.

I always loved playing outside in our small garden and my father fixed a wooden swing on a lower branch of the sycamore tree and that was enjoyed for years. When Susan Baker moved into the street when I was about four, at last I had a playmate and we would spend hours on the swing, or trotting up and down the street 'dressed up' in various princess outfits. The skirts were usually made from old curtains simply gathered round the waist and

45

secured by a belt. They had to be long, and they had to be very swirly. An old handbag was sometimes cadged to complete the outfit, although I never remember tottering round in high heels.

The tiny garden shed was taken over as a substitute for a 'Wendy House.' We had a couple of old plates and would collect things to make a pretend 'meal'. Mud was fashioned into various shapes, and leaves were collected to represent other items of food – not always vegetables! For reasons maybe never known to me, plantain leaves were used to represent bacon, and sorrel leaves were duly collected and gingerly munched on for real: they have rather a pleasant taste of vinegar.

I don't think I ever showed much interest in the two large dolls that I remember, Pauline and Christine. My interest in dolls came later, when I was eight or nine. But skipping was a great game. It could be played alone, or if you could find two other girls to hold a longer rope, a great time could be had, with many simple rhyming songs to accompany, like *blue bells, cockle shells, eevie, ivy, over*, or *salt, vinegar, mustard, pepper*, where the turning became faster and faster, until you tripped to a stop. Of course, you had to wait until the washing line snapped to get the rope in the first place.

One Christmas, when I was about five, I received an umbrella! It was snowing outside, and I spent the whole day walking up and down the street in my wellies, enchanted.

Sweets were on ration during my early years and my mother

would take the coupons to the corner shop every Friday morning, when she got her 'order'. There might be a penny bar of Cadbury's chocolate, or 'floral gums' or Pontefract Cakes – still a favourite of mine. Liquorice was always known as 'spanish', and could be bought in many forms: shoelaces, wheels or bars with a flattened end. These could be dipped into 'kali', a powdered sherbet, and sucked. Kali was very tangy and left you with a yellow tongue, as did gobstoppers, which could leave you with a tongue of any colour: pink, blue or green. If I ever got my hands on a Mars Bar, it was carefully sliced into eight or nine sections, and each piece savoured separately making it last a whole day.

In 1953 I discovered bubble gum. Suddenly on display at the corner shop was a small packet called 'Wow', and at a penny a time, you got a small pink square of gum and a tiny photograph: 'Favourites of the Stars'! At that time I had never been to the cinema, but I had seen pictures in magazines and the exotic names thrilled me: Pier Angeli, Cyd Charisse, Van Johnson. Of course another collection was started and eventually these miniature photographs – less than an inch square – were put into an album. Swaps were made all over the street and eventually I was only one missing to complete the set. Gene Kelly finally turned up on a railway station platform somewhere in Wales, as we were wending our way to Tenby, rather trodden on, but seized upon with glee. I don't think I ever touched bubble gum after that; I must have chewed my way through a hundred packets.

Some time in the summer of 1954 I became very ill with scarlet fever. I was in bed for six weeks, very poorly and unable to keep down the new penicillin medicine that the doctor had given me. My father was banished to the bed in the box room while my poor mother nursed me day and night, and as I started to recover, keep up with my constant demands for amusement. It was at this time that she brought me a book that yielded a cardboard doll and pages and pages of 'outfits' that had to be cut out and fastened to the doll's shoulders and waist with paper tabs. A tiny pair of scissors was provided and I sat for days, fascinated, giving my mother some well-earned respite. It was so successful that she then found me a similar book with a pixie and friend to be dressed in paper outfits, which was even more exciting. Of course, she was reading to me every day and I had paper and crayons to keep me occupied.

At the end of the six weeks, I found that I was too weak to walk, so that had to be learned all over again. In those days, following an infection of scarlet fever, the house had to be fumigated and the whole family was told to remove themselves from the premises while this was done. Fortunately for me, the time coincided with the release of Walt Disney's *Peter Pan* at the pictures, and my brother, who would have then been almost eighteen, took me to see it. I can't ever remember going to the pictures before that and, of course, from then on I became a great fan of everything Disney. A *Peter Pan* book was procured, probably for my birthday in September, along with a *Peter Pan* jigsaw. I sat in one of the armchairs in the front room, a tray placed across the arms and another delightful discovery was made. Over the months I collected almost all the old Disney stories in jigsaw form, my favourite being the *Walrus and the Carpenter* from *Alice in Wonderland*. I loved the innocent faces on the row of baby oysters being lined up for dinner!

I was sitting on this chair, the tray in front of me and reading a copy of my mother's *Woman's Own*, when I found out the shocking truth about Father Christmas. I must have been able to read fairly well, or at least better than my mother thought I could, as I found an article about finding the right time to break the news that Father Christmas didn't exist.

'There is no Father Christmas, is there?' I asked my mother. The shock on her face told me it was true. I took it well, looking back. There were no tears, perhaps I had already worked it out. It hadn't helped when, one Christmas Eve a couple of years before, a doll's house had been put at the side of my parent's bed in preparation for the morning and my father, getting up groggily in the dark during the night, had tripped up over it and badly stubbed his toes. The resulting shout and cursing woke me and I was out of bed like a shot. 'Has he been?' It was clear that he had been, but I was told he was coming back later with the rest of my presents. I wasn't convinced. Also, on running downstairs, the reindeers hadn't taken their mince pies. Definitely something fishy going on.

When did I get my kaleidoscope? Probably around this time,

maybe the same Christmas, but I had no idea when I lifted the unpromising tube to my eye and turned the end what joy it would bring me. It was truly like magic, a wonderful trick that I could perform to transform these tiny pieces of coloured glass into such beautiful patterns. It must have kept me quiet for hours and I never tired of it.

My mother came back from the corner shop one day in 1954 with a packet of Brooke Bond tea. She opened the packet and handed me a small picture card of a bird called a fieldfare, which I had never heard of, but it was an exquisite miniature artwork of a beautiful bird perched on a branch covered with berries and another passion was born. I don't think I ever had an album to put them in, but they were treasured, as were the new series of wild flowers that followed.

It was a good job that about that time my brother had married and moved out of the house, giving me the much larger back bedroom, still with the old sideboard in place to keep my collections in.

Plasticine was much in favour in those days and a new packet with bright new colours was always appreciated. Sometimes the colours became mixed and ended up in a ball of sludgy brown – a great lesson for when I started painting and learning to mix my colours. Plasticine plates were fashioned and tiny pieces of green plasticine rolled to make peas. Eggs were made from yellow and white, red sausages rolled, mashed potato moulded. I was never much good at figures or animals, but had a bash at making a farmyard scene once.

One day Susan Baker's older brother, Philip, appeared in the street on a three-wheel bike. Suddenly, he was my new best friend. I had always wanted a bike, but there was never enough money to buy one, but I loved hurtling down the street, which was quite steep, and begged a 'go' whenever I saw him outside. Kids came from all around to take turns and his parents must have been horrified to see this new bike being given such a bashing. We probably wore it out in a few weeks.

By this time I had learned to knit and sew, so dolls began to

49

dominate the scene. Small scarves were knitted and my mother helped me to cut out and sew tiny dresses and jackets for them. Any scrap of fabric was coveted and I remember receiving a precious remnant of ice blue brocade, embroidered all over with silver flowers that had been used by one of our neighbours for a wedding outfit. It came along with a strip of white cotton daisies that had been used to trim it. The resulting creation, although a bit stiff for a small doll, transformed her into a fairy princess. Although I played endlessly with my dolls until I was about eleven, I can't remember a single name I gave them, although I'm sure they had them. I spent a lot of time with Joan, my friend from school, and we each had a small cardboard suitcase full of doll's clothes. For some reason we were particularly keen that our dolls had 'travelling suits', although, of course, they never went anywhere.

Paints and crayons were always in good supply and at some stage I got a toy typewriter. The letters were on a dial that had to be swizzled round to the right position, a tedious procedure, but it eventually produced acceptable results on the paper. It stood me in good staid later when I started work, as, without Tippex in use at that time, accuracy was essential.

When I was about ten I started to 'publish' a newspaper with my friend Joan. This work was done in the shed and the resulting tabloid– there was only one copy per edition – was called *The Bluebird News*. Pictures and snippets of news and fashion were culled from women's magazines and catalogues and stuck on the paper with glue. We put in our own news items as well, such as *Mr. Trengove has some new fish in his pond*, or *Mrs. Wood's cat has eaten her budgie* – big news, that was.

One thing is certain, along with wandering the fields and ponds every fine day to collect wild flowers and reading every day, I was never short of something to do. Not a single one of my 'toys' required a battery or a plug and I still believe that to be brought up as a child in the 1950s was the very best time in the world.

I shall have to delve very deep to the back of my memory's filing cabinet to retrieve this folder: my first days at school.

But what's this? The first page is missing altogether and a lot of the other pages are ravaged by time. I shall just have to do my best.

I first went to All Saints' infant's school in September 1950, a couple of weeks before my fourth birthday. My brother was much older than I was and had been of no use whatsoever as a playmate, and tots of my own age had been in short supply, so I must have been overwhelmed by the great crowd of children assembled in my first classroom. It was probably the biggest room I had ever seen, having to hold almost forty pupils, as they did in those days and it appeared a monstrous size to me.

My first teacher was Mrs Holt, a tall lady, although not tall enough to open the high windows: she needed a long pole with a hook on the end to do that. I was shown something called a 'cloakroom' where I was to leave my coat, on a peg which had a picture above it, to make it easier to remember. I was asked if I had brought any 'lunch' with me, which I hadn't; another mysterious concept.

The classroom was a sea of tiny desks and chairs and the rest of the space was taken up by a huge rocking horse, a wendy house and dozens of toys to keep us occupied. It was chaos. At break time we were given bottles of milk to drink, something that I flatly refused to do, and it took a visit from my mother to convince Mrs Holt that I never touched the stuff. I always went home for dinner – the school was scarcely much more than a hundred yards from my house – then in the afternoons we all went into the next room, where camp beds were laid out and we were supposed to have our 'afternoon nap,' although I suspect this was done more for the teachers' benefit than ours. Not many of us ever went to sleep.

It was in this room that we did all our exercise and dance to the accompaniment of music by Mrs Holt at the piano. We also learned simple songs, all long forgotten. In fact, my clearest recollection of being in Mrs Holt's class was the day that she put me on her knee at her desk, opened a drawer and pulled out a tin. This was opened to reveal a small pair of scissors. 'If you don't stop chattering, I will cut your tongue off with these scissors!' she said. It didn't work.

In general, though, I liked Mrs Holt very much and enjoyed my days at school, but without a photograph to aid my 'memory file' most of the detail has been lost.

I moved 'up' to Mrs Lilley's class after a couple of years and my memory serves me rather better here, much aided by the fact that there are *two* class photographs. One of these has a placard on the front desk stating that it was 'Coronation Year – 1953', with a picture of the Queen, so no doubt about that one.

Mrs Lilley stands proudly in the background, having for once managed to get all thirty-nine of her pupils seated neatly at their desks with a (mostly) beaming smile on their face. We all got some kind of special gift for the Coronation celebrations, but I can only remember a pencil.

Mrs Lilley was a stout lady with the obligatory hair roll in the post war years fashion, severely pinned into place. She was elderly and wore frumpy clothes and clumpy shoes. She was probably about thirty-nine.

She loved to tell us tales of derring-do involving her grandfather, who was captain of the Cutty Sark, the famous tea clipper. And she taught us the miracle of growing cress on wet blotting paper.

There was much ado with wax crayons and crepe paper, especially at Christmas, when we all made cards for our parents and paper chains for the classroom. In the photograph I am poised with a small pair of scissors, cutting pictures from magazine pages. On the walls there are alphabet pictures: 'g is for Girl who is mopping the floor' – we were firmly put in our place early on. The 'b for boy' is out of the shot. I would love to see it.

In the wintertime we grew bulbs in clear glass bottles to watch the white roots growing longer every day and there are various renditions in pencil of the resulting blooms pinned on the wall at the back. I remember in winter it was unbearably cold sometimes. Even though it was such a short journey to the school doors, I used to cry with frozen fingers and toes. At times like that we all did special exercises to warm us up before lessons started: mostly stamping our feet up and down and shaking our fingers until the tingling stopped.

Looking round the class we were generally a clean, tidy group of good looking kids, although Stewart Taylor was already showing signs of becoming the handsomest. And Georgie Barlow signs of criminal tendencies. I notice I am sitting opposite Joan, my new best friend. My straight blonde hair has been curled at the bottom with curling pins, which I had in every night, and two ribbons tie up bunches.

School was mostly play at that time and I have no recollection whatsoever of learning anything, but I must have done, because by the time I moved up to the junior class, I could read and write, do sums and identify all the pink bits on the world map.

Life was a lot tougher in Mrs McMaster's class. Even the threat of scissors hadn't stopped me chattering incessantly, and more than once I was obliged to stand on a chair to have a ruler applied to the back of my legs. (Mrs McMasters was even older than Mrs Lilley and had trouble bending down to near-floor level to administer slaps.) On the class photograph (1954?) I am sitting next to Stewart Taylor, my dreamboat. The walls are completely covered in pictures: children playing in the snow, a pirate ship captained by a duck, the Pied Piper and a list of words that rhyme with 'sail' – mail, pail, nail etc.

This is where the girls first had needlework lessons. My mother had bought a length of cream cotton cloth covered with rosebuds. It was duly cut out from a pattern to make me an underskirt. I thought it was beautiful, but we only had a couple of lessons a week and by the time it was finished, with the fussy French seams,

I had grown so much it didn't fit me. I don't know who was more upset, me or my mother.

All Saints' was closely connected to All Saints' Church, a few hundred yards down the road on the A6 and it was in Mrs McMaster's class that we started to attend services there on special occasions like Ash Wednesday and Easter. We were all lined up outside and walked in a long unruly 'crocodile' down the road. I, being brought up a heathen, had never been in a church before and was overawed by the splendour of it. I loved the whole ritual of the service and we sang 'There is a green hill far away,' and 'All things bright and beautiful,' with great gusto even if we never gave a single thought to the meanings of the words. I remember the Harvest Festival services, when we all had to take a box of fruit and vegetables to donate to the needy and we sang 'We plough the fields and scatter...' We were given small religious picture cards to keep and bribed to come back every week to collect a set. Despite pleas to my parents, I only ever went to church with the school, which wasn't often. Christmastime was best and we practised the carols for weeks before, Mrs McMasters giving a decent performance on the piano in the hall. We even learned to barn-dance.

Mr Lewis' class was next, and probably the one I have the least recollection of, except that his preferred method of chastisement was to make you 'stand in the corner.' There was no dunce's hat, but it was implied. The comment on my report read: 'Judith's failing is that she is such a chatterbox...' So I was still at it.

As I was still, when I moved up to Mr Howarth's class, the 'top class' - so I must have been about ten by that time. Mr Howarth was the headmaster and his preferred method of chastisement was the cane.

I have a class photograph for this one, and I'm sitting at the front with a new hairstyle. The bunches and ribbons are gone and I have a plain, short bob that looks as if it has been done with a pudding basin. It probably had; I never then, as now, went to a hairdresser. And there she is! Rhona Peverley, the bane of my life for the few months until I left, sitting next to my best friend, Joan. Rhona had recently moved into the area when she joined the school and she immediately took control of our little clique. She insisted that she join Joan and myself in our shed 'meetings'. She poured scorn on our 'password' entry and our attempts to produce our own newspaper, the *Bluebird News*; she didn't play with dolls and would arrive with a pocketful of coins, stolen from her mother's purse. She urged us to do likewise, which we both flatly refused to do, but she did eventually persuade Joan to take her Post Office savings book and withdraw ten shillings. I don't know what they did with it.

We were gearing up to the eleven plus examinations and one morning Mr Howarth had to attend to something important so he left one of the boys (Michael Bloore, I've never forgiven him) in charge with the instruction: 'If anyone talks, write their name on the blackboard!' In the ensuing ten minutes, Michael managed to write about fifteen names on the blackboard, whether a crime had been perpetrated or not – including mine. And, difficult as it may be to believe, I had not uttered a word. Mr Howarth returned, furious, and the accused were ordered to line up to be caned. He disregarded the several pleas of, 'But it wasn't me, Sir!' A line was formed and we were all duly caned. Justice had not been done, but in hindsight, I reckoned that I must have got away with talking out of turn a hundred times without punishment, so I guess it was due.

Although I didn't cry when he did it, I cried all the way home at dinnertime, I was so ashamed. I told my mother that I had banged my hand on a wall to explain the redness and the tears.

It was probably some time into the New Year of 1958 when Joan's mother died. Asian flu had swept through the land and, although she was only in her early thirties, she didn't have the strength to survive it. So dear, sweet, gentle Joan lost her mother and the shock of the news devastated us all.

The eleven plus exams went ahead regardless, and Joan, a bright girl who should have passed, was left with most of the others to go to Birch Road, the local secondary modern. In fact, out of the whole class of thirty-odd, only two of us passed – myself and Stewart Taylor, a shocking result that Mr Howarth should have been ashamed of.

All Saints' was not a good school, but I was fortunate to move on unscathed and went to the brand new, pretentiously named, Worsley Wardley Grammar School, which was only a couple of hundred yards from my house in the opposite direction. But that's another story…

NATURE GIRL

My earliest memories were mostly times of discovery, the kind of discovery that only a small child can make: their first sight of a scuttling beetle, a jar of sticklebacks proudly displayed by the boy next door, a book with colourful pictures of fairy princesses and pixies, the iridescent glory of a butterfly. But the most beautiful things for me were flowers: the improbable faces of pansies; the first time my mother showed me a bee finding the secret door in a snapdragon; the simple magic of the first primrose I ever saw, growing wild on the 'top field'.

In a lot of ways I had a magical childhood. Even though there were no other children of my age in our street, I have always been contented to amuse myself alone, and I don't ever remember being bored; as now, I never seemed to have enough time. We lived in Wardley, which at that time was a row of four short streets off the A6. At the top of the street was a patch of rough ground with (what seemed at the time) a large pond and beyond that, farmers' fields that stretched back for ever. So the 'top field' was where I spent most of my days. Even the smallest children were allowed to play out unattended and without fear at that time, so kitted out in my tiny wellies and clutching a hopeful jam jar I trotted off up the street to the pond, where I was enchanted by the teeming pond life, trying, thankfully without a great deal of success, to capture darting newts or little silver fish or water bugs. I would stay up there for hours, wading in from the edge, a little bit further and a little bit further, until the pond water surged over the top of my wellies, and I knew I would be in big trouble – again - when I got home. And, sure enough, I would be plonked on the draining board where the squelching wellies were dragged off, then the soaking, slightly muddy socks, accompanied by much 'chunnering' by my mother. But the pond was a magnet and I never learned to resist it.

I was blessed to live in a house where there were always books and I was given, very early on, the precious gift of a set of Flower Fairy books which I pored over for hours, quickly learning that the flowers growing so freely on the top field had such beautiful names as rose-bay-willow-herb, tansy, toadflax, herb Robert, vetch, and the astoundingly-named bird's-foot-trefoil, although I never found the scarlet spire of berries of a lords-and-ladies plant. Specimens were duly collected and put into cups of water when I got home. In my memory, it was always summer and every day was full of sunshine and pleasure.

But my most joyful memory was the day when I arrived home from school to find a kitten. My mother had never been very fond of cats but she had come down into the kitchen one morning to find that a frying-pan, left on the top of the stove and containing a substantial layer of bacon dripping, was criss-crossed by the patter of tiny feet. It was more than obvious that some brave mouse pioneer had discovered this tasty treat and gone back to fetch the rest of the family. It didn't take much to horrify my mother at the best of times, so there was quite a kerfuffle at this discovery. A kitten was swiftly procured, although I recall no discussion of it at the time, so it was with total surprise and amazement that I discovered this enchanting creature, as wide-eyed with wonder as I was, peeping up from a cardboard box. The innocent joy of realising that this exquisite creature had come to live with us was never quite surpassed.

I swept it up into my arms, its baby blue eyes looking into my face with astonishment. On finding out that it was a boy, I promptly named him Tibby and I spent the next few years completely in his thrall. He soon discarded the cardboard box and took over the sofa for his bed. He would tear around the house, light as a feather, running up the curtains with ease, darting along the back of a chair, spitting in his excitement, performing acrobatics with a piece of string, then suddenly his saucer eyes would droop closed, his little head would flop and he would be fast asleep, giving me ample leisure to examine his tiny shell-pink paw pads, bordered with deadly curved needles; the delightful design of his moist little nose where it joined onto his mouth with its set of miniature shark's teeth; the downy hair lining his perfect ears; his tiny tail like a piece of fluffy string. His clumsy attempts to wash his face sent us all into paroxysms of delight. Tibby was a fawn-coloured tiger-stripy cat, a bit like a ginger tom who had been through the wash a few times too many and he was a small bundle of pure joy.

He never became cross, however much I cuddled and fussed over him and even my mother became enamoured when he discovered that she had the comfiest knee in the house and she spent hours combing his fur while he purred like a train, kneading her legs with his growing claws. He eventually became so big that, as a five-year old, I could hardly pick him up, but pick him up I did, sometimes tucking him into my doll's pram and taking him for a walk down the street. He took it all so good-naturedly, only drawing the line when I put my doll's bonnet on his head. But he enjoyed being wheeled out in the pram and the only time he ever jumped out was when I had put my doll's matinee jacket on him. It fitted quite well – dolls at that time were often large, pot affairs made to look like real babies, and Pauline – as mine was called – had quite an array of home-made clothes. Tibby was fine for a while, then suddenly leapt out of the pram and off he went up the street, his front legs encased in the sleeves of the matinee jacket, trotting awkwardly, but at a faster pace than I could muster, and it was a good hour before he returned home, minus jacket, demanding a late lunch. We never found out how he had freed himself of the offending vestment and he flatly refused to tell us, but after that his pram-pushed days were over.

But the mice never reappeared and I adored Tibby until he was very sadly run over and killed four years later. And, although I was never quite on a par with Gerald Durrell, my love of nature gave me an enchanted childhood, and stays with me to this very day as I sit out in my garden, locked down with the rest of the world. I realise my great good fortune that I am surrounded by flowers and trees, as so many are not, and this adds a layer of sadness to the joy that I still feel watching the tadpoles swishing round my pond, the wonder of watching a robin and a goldfinch drinking together in my birdbath and the bees disappear through that secret door in a snap-dragon.

MEMORIES OF MY MOTHER

My father was a very keen photographer so I have dozens of photographs of my mother when she was young. She usually looked happy and carefree; a face I rarely saw when I was growing up. Many of them were probably taken between 1930 and 1945; a few years before I was born, at any rate. She must have been quite a looker in her teens because I remember her once telling me that she had been engaged three times before she met my father – and they were married when she was twenty! There were photographs of her posed, dressed in a Japanese kimono outfit; in a Spanish head-dress with a fan and a lovely picture of her in a blue taffeta ball gown. All artistically posed with the lighting carefully arranged, especially the scantily-attired pictures, an acute source of embarrassment to me as much now as they were when I first saw them.

She was born in 1913, almost the youngest of ten children, and although she was intelligent and artistic, she had to leave school at fourteen to 'work in the mill' to help support the family. She worked there until she married and my brother was born in 1934.

The war years were fairly kind to my parents, in that my father, who had hearing problems and worked in what was deemed to be an 'essential' service, wasn't away from home and my mother worked at Burtons, in Wardley where they lived, sewing uniforms for the forces. My brother, lived with his grandmother during the week while my parents were working, leaving them free to spend time together; to go to the pictures; to go out dancing, which they loved, and money would not have been as scarce as it was later after I was born and my mother had to give up work. In a way, these were probably the best years of her life. She loved her work and had a lot of friends at Burtons, so it was a great shock to her when I came along, unbidden, in 1946. She became a reluctant mother and housewife and never worked again.

My mother scrubbed the kitchen floor the day she died, because it was a Wednesday.

She had become a woman of rigid routine: she did the washing on a Monday, the ironing on a Tuesday and on a Thursday she cleaned the front windows and donkey-stoned the front step, whether it was raining or not. The lovely floral curtains (home-made, of course, and without linings) were always hung with the pattern on the outside, so they looked good from the street. We lived with the 'ghost' of the pattern and seams on the inside. She could be the most dreadful snob at times.

Meals were also tightly regulated: lamb chops for Saturday lunch – although we called it 'dinner', of course; a very small roast joint on a Sunday and because there was never anything left over for 'left-overs', corned beef hash on a Monday, when she did her washing. Washing was quite a palaver in the late forties. We had no washing machine so it was all done in the large stone sink, except for big items like sheets and towels, when a large metal 'tub' was brought in from the shed. It was filled with scalding water and soap powder, then what she called a 'poncher' was pressed into service – something like an inverted copper colander fixed onto a long wooden handle that was vigorously applied to thrash the clothes into submission.

When I was very small, most of the cooking was done in the oven built into the fireplace in the front room – it produced rice puddings I have never since tasted the like of – but we had an electric hotplate with two rings in the kitchen. Here she produced a magnificent chicken broth from simply clear stock, carrot and onion but with a delicious flavour I have never been able to replicate. If we had a chicken, which was rare, it was always a 'boiler', a roast chicken reserved for Christmas day or very special occasions. The 'boiler' was cooked in a pressure cooker that my father had won in a photographic competition around 1950, but I don't think she ever cooked one without exclaiming, 'It's a tough bugger, this is!'

Seventy years later and I still use the base of the pressure cooker to make all my soup, a not infrequent occurrence.

Toast was done on a toasting fork in front of the fire – a task always performed by my father. I still like it black. Presumably we had a lot of 'salads' in the summer, when there was no fire needed, although these never ventured much from lettuce, tomato and cucumber with boiled ham or very occasionally a tin of salmon. With, of course, Heinz Salad Cream.

During the most severe periods of rationing in the late 'forties, from time to time we might receive a food parcel from my mother's sister, my Auntie May, who lived in Canada. Apparently, just after the First World War, around 1919, my grandfather decided that the whole family would emigrate to Canada and all preparations were made for the journey, including selling up half the furniture.

The four eldest children May, Phyllis, Ernest and Tom, who would have all been in their late teens or early twenties – had gone over first to prepare a home for them all. I never found out quite what happened, except that my grandfather changed his mind at the last minute and decided to stay in England. The four pioneers were enjoying their life in Canada so much that they all decided to stay over there, and so the family was split.

My mother, who would have been six at the time, missed her sisters very much and they kept in contact until the 1960s when we seemed to lose track of them. But during the worst times of austerity in the late forties and early fifties, from time to time a cardboard box stuffed with goodies would arrive from Canada, and it would be like Christmas for a couple of weeks.

There would always be tins of ham, sliced peaches, corned beef, probably the ubiquitous tin of Spam. There would be packets of tea and *real* coffee – not the liquid chicory substitute stuff called 'Camp' which my mother hated. There were rare ingredients for baking, like raisins, desiccated coconut and dried egg; a whole box full of treats, and on one occasion, a strange cardboard package that was labelled 'Mary Baker Gingerbread Cake Mix'! We had never seen anything like it in this country and I can still remember the delicious taste when I scraped the bowl.

My mother had a rich store of what I presume to have been local sayings: for instance, ever disappointed with my fine, sparse, hair she would say, while tugging it into some semblance of order, 'I've seen better hair on bacon!' If a knife had become blunt and needed sharpening – my father's job of course - she would loudly complain 'You could ride bare-arsed to Yorkshire on that bugger!' That would usually get the job done.

Although she was a reluctant mother – and never let me forget it – I think she enjoyed having a little girl to dress up. She was, as almost all women were in those days, a skilled seamstress and made just about every item of clothing that I possessed from my first days. A lot of my dresses had a smocked front that she worked at on a wooden frame that my father had made for her. The silks were wound on stiff cardboard bobbins and the colours had special names, like peach or rose or midnight blue, which sounded very exotic to me as a small child. I still possess the remnants of her collection to this day.

She endlessly knitted cardigans and jumpers, a notable example being a white cardigan with a blue willow-pattern design all over it – quite a feat at the best of times. I think it was 1954, when I would have been seven and unfortunately, this intricate activity coincided with the Wimbledon final on the television where her favourite, Jaroslav Drobny was playing against Ken Rosewall and down to a nail-biting fourth set. It was already eight games to seven in Drobny's favour, but with Rosewall to serve. Knit eight blue, purl five white, wool forward; and on the court, 'Deuce!!!' was called for the ninth time. I chose this moment to rush in from the garden with two bloodied knees, scraped after a fall on the path and blubbing like a baby. A stitch was dropped. 'Advantage Rosewall!' My mother could swear like a trouper at times and that was one of those times.

The cardigan was never finished because by the time the first sleeve was completed, I had already outgrown it and it barely reached my elbow.

Although my mother never really liked children and always bemoaned my appearance into her life, she always made sure that she did her 'duty' and although there was a whiff of the burning martyr about her, she always treated me kindly, looked after all my needs and above all, she always read to me. A great lover of reading herself – her especial favourites being historical novels, like those of Jean Plaidy - she encouraged a love of books which has never left me.

It was all a different story, however, when my daughter was born in 1966. There has probably never been a more doting grandmother. She fussed and fretted over her in a way she had never done with me, and she was adored in return. I can just imagine them now, my daughter cuddled to her side, while my mother read a fairytale to her, just the way my grandmother had read to me.

My mother died, very suddenly, in 1974, at the age of 61; I was twenty-seven. She was one of those countless millions of women over the ages who have led unfulfilled lives, governed by uncontrolled child-bearing. Philip Larkin said that 'Sex began in 1964' with the advent of 'The Pill'; he could have said that that was the year when women gained control over their lives and finally started to spread their wings.

THE JOY OF READING

Some of my earliest memories are of sitting in bed with my grandmother whilst she read to me. She lived with us for a few years around the time that I was born just after the war, taking up residence in the 'back bedroom' while my then-teenaged brother was confined to the tiny box room. I slept in a cot in my parents' room – just about until I outgrew it when I was almost three.

Every morning a plate of buttered toast and Rose's lime marmalade was taken up to Grannie, along with a copy of the Daily Express and I would snuggle in beside her, cadging bits of toast while she read to me the adventures of Rupert Bear. There would be frequent pleas from her to, 'Ooo, mind me bad leg!' as I fidgeted and wriggled about at her side but I quickly became hooked on comic strips, and never looked back.

As I outgrew the cot, my grandmother moved out to live with my uncle and I took over the box room from my brother, whilst my mother took over the comic strip duties.

Our 'corner shop' only sold basic items like bread and milk, tea and sugar, potatoes and carrots, so twice a week my mother would walk into Swinton from Wardley where we lived, to do the more specialised shopping. There was a fishmonger's, where I first saw the tidy rows of gleaming, glassy-eyed herring and cod with the wonder of iridescent scales. There was a butcher's shop, (Chappells) where much activity went on behind the bustling counter, with vigorous chopping and slicing to be observed while waiting in the long queue to be served with our lamb chops and bacon. The chemist shop was exciting with its strange smells and gleaming coloured glass bottles, where we would emerge with cough medicine, Elastoplast for scraped knees or pills for my mother's headaches.

But most exciting of all was the newsagent's shop where we went to buy the latest copy of *Sunny Stories*, a whole miniature magazine full of tales of pixies and elves; puppy dogs and kittens; small children, just like me, having exciting adventures. It was tuppence and I could scarcely contain my excitement until we got home and my mother would read it to me from cover to cover. Each copy would be carefully stored away to be brought out time after time – treasured possessions – and the start of my life-long habit of collecting.

Swiftly following the *Sunny Stories* were comics like *Beano* and *Dandy*, now mixed in my memory so that I'm not sure whether Desperate Dan appeared in the one or the other, and the same applied to Dennis the Menace, Korky the Kat and the infamous Roger the Dodger. They were the first comics to make use of 'speech balloons' for the dialogue, and, sitting by my mother day after day, I think I must have absorbed the art of reading by some kind of osmosis. I certainly have no recollection of having been formally taught, either at home or at school. The collections of these precious items were stored in a huge (well, it seemed that way when I was four) dark oak sideboard left behind in my grandmother's room when she left, and the magazines pored over so many times that they probably fell to pieces in the end.

It might have been a Christmas when I received my first Noddy book: *Noddy in Toyland*, and from then on I became one of Enid Blyton's most ardent fans. I adored that little fellow and his improbable companions, quite unaware that he was a misogynistic, homosexual racist who has long since been cast into political exile. He even dared to poke fun at Big Ears' big ears!

It's such a shame that children today can't be delighted by these lovable characters – Tessie Bear, Bumpy Dog and Mr Plod, along with various mischievous Golliwogs, but fortunately for me at the time, despite money always being in short supply, somehow books were listed high on the agenda of priorities and the beginnings of my lifelong library were assembled.

I started my next collection when I received *two* Famous Five books one Christmas. I don't recall how old I was, but I remember that my mother was dismayed when I read the first one right through on Christmas day. 'They won't last long,' she said. She needn't have worried – they were all re-read over and over through the next few years as I thrilled to the mad-cap adventures of Julian, Dick, Anne, George and their dog, Timmy. These were much more grown-up than the Noddy books and the pixies and fairies that had filled my younger years, but now I envied the Famous Five their exciting exploits, especially when a picnic was involved. I had never been taken on a picnic and relished the accounts of cucumber sandwiches, sticky buns and, always, lashings of lemonade – particularly the lashings of lemonade, which I thought would be the very height of grown-up sophistication.

Clearly, looking back, Julian was a bit gay and George, the tom-boy, was clearly on the way to a gender re-assignment, but at the time I innocently adored them all and all but wore them out with my continual readings.

The next discovery was the Secret Seven, another Enid Blyton creation of child detectives. They led an even more exciting life that the Famous Five, meeting in a secluded shed, and only allowed admittance by displaying their 'SS' badge and giving the correct password! They had a *password*! This was a new concept swiftly adopted by myself and my new best friend, Joan. I sat next to Joan at school but she lived 'across the road': the not-so-busy-then A6 at Wardley, so it wasn't so easy to play together without the assistance of an adult, but I had a garden shed for the 'meetings' which was pressed into service, and it was there that we plotted our 'investigations'.

We would roam the streets, looking for anything suspicious, any kind of 'mystery' we could solve. Once we found the hoof-prints of a horse in some mud and tracked them until they ran out in the grass field at the top of the street – clearly someone was up to no good! Could there be gypsies? On one occasion we spied a large number of small cardboard boxes on the back seat of a car parked at the top of the street – a rarity in itself as almost no-one had a car in those days. There was clearly smuggling going on here, or even worse, they could have been the loot from a robbery. We arranged to investigate further by meeting 'in the night' – a time of half past ten was agreed – when we could creep up to the car and hide to see if the 'smuggler' came out and provided any more clues. I stayed awake until I heard my parents go up to bed then crept down the creaking stairs into the hall. I silently opened the front door and peered out into the darkness. There was not a soul around. I decided the time wasn't *quite* right and went back to bed to wait another half an hour. Unfortunately, I nodded off as soon as my head hit the pillow and we never found out what heinous crimes had been committed at the top of the street.

The leader of Enid Blyton's Secret Seven was Peter, an awful bully who thought nothing of reducing the girls to tears if they forgot the password, or otherwise just behaved like soppy girls do. Probably he's been banned as well now, but I feel blessed that I had the chance to read all these wonderful stories.

Somewhere along the line, my parents bought an entire set of children's encyclopaedias: Newnes *Pictorial Knowledge*. Ten volumes of pure delight, covering every aspect of the world that any child could ever want to know about: 'Romance of History', 'The Story of the Human Body', 'The Kingdom of the Seas'. Lavishly illustrated, there were colour plates showing flags of the world, different gemstones, British birds; so much to fill any rainy day. But my favourite section was 'A Children's Treasury of Verse.' Beautifully illustrated, it was here that I learned 'The Owl and the Pussycat', 'Home-Thoughts from Abroad' by Robert Browning and 'There was a Naughty Boy' by Keats (which I can still recite, if pushed).

Looking back, they were gloriously politically incorrect. The section on 'A Guide to Good Manners for Boys and Girls' contains such gems as: 'If a lady drops something in public, a gentleman will at once pick it up for her, raising his hat as he hands it back,' 'A gentleman should always give his arm to an elderly lady when walking with her,' – 'elderly' probably meaning sixty plus.

There was a section for handicrafts: 'It is important to remember that if a child allows his hands to grow up useless he will never be able to train them afterwards.'(!) There were instructions to make model ships, kites and a simple electric motor – for boys, of course, and instructions to knit, sew and embroider for girls, together with diagrams to make a weaving frame in cardboard (best left to a brother if one available). There is a lovely pattern for girls to make an apron, probably a good idea as she would be wearing one the rest of her life.

These encyclopaedias were my treasured possessions and it was with horror that I watched my mother pass them on to my brother's children, who were barely past toddler stage, watching helplessly as pages were torn out and beloved stories scribbled on. They very quickly hit the bin. I mourned their loss for years until 1995 when I was on a cottage holiday somewhere in Cumbria. I wandered into a second-hand book shop and found a whole set for sale. I had just been made redundant and money was tight, but I would have gone without shoes for a year to get them, and so they were brought back home to take up their rightful place in my collection, where I still get great pleasure in perusing their pages from time to time.

Of course there were my favourite Flower Fairy books; Alice in Wonderland and Peter Pan; endless Enid Blyton books of fairy tales and the adventures of Malory Towers but by the time I was about ten I had moved on to the classics. *The Secret Garden* and *Little Women* were great favourites, but one birthday I requested

Black Beauty, by Anna Sewell as a present, only to discover that my friend Joan, whose birthday was very close to mine, had requested the same thing. So we solemnly exchanged carefully wrapped copies to each other of identical books. We were both very happy with this arrangement.

Tragically, early the following year – 1957 – Joan's mother died in the Asian flu' epidemic. She had been a healthy young woman, probably no more than in her early thirties, and it seemed that our carefree childhood years had come to an abrupt end.

In 1956 my father had joined the Companion Book Club, a fairly new concept in those days. One book a month was delivered – no choice in the selection – but soon the oak bookcase in the living room was full of thrillers, mysteries and adventure novels, together with WW11 memoirs like *Reach for the Sky* by Douglas Bader and *Boldness be my Friend* by Richard Pape, the latter being the account of three years in a German prisoner of war camp. *The Surprise of Cremona* by Edith Templeton was my first, but by no means last, experience of armchair travel.

I suppose these books were my introduction into adult reading and as I look round my house now, sixty years on, with every room crammed with books, every flat surface supporting its own untidy pile of paperbacks, reading continues to be one of my dearest interests to this day.

Street & Parlour Games

Bouncing two balls against gable walls
Farmer's in his den – picked as a hen
Go-kart given wings to fly - pie in sky
Hula hoops and Frisbee swoops
Icy slide made by kids caused many skids
Larger bag rattles if winning marble battles
Noisy fun with a cap-filled gun
Pattern swirling on whipped top whirring
Plank & crate, seesaw rides elate
Push a dolly in a trolley
Rip-raps on Bonfire Night give a fright
Roller Skates with extended plates
Rope for skipping or lamppost swinging
Hopscotch on flags wiped out with rags
Snowman dropped brush when turned to slush
Tick-and-you're-it, scatter very quick
Tug of war between rival streets, using sheets
When lamplighter came, end of any game

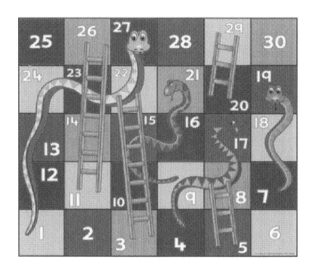

Building a tent with chairs and a blanket
Cards played: Snap, Happy Families & Old Maid
Comics read with hilarity and glee
Drumming band with spoons and pans
Go to a nook with torch and a book
'Hangman' losses and noughts & crosses
'I went to market', alphabetically from A to Z
Knocking down rows of snaking dominoes
Musical Bumps and Simon says "jump"
Oranges & Lemons arch or Duke of York march
Painting clothes pegs – faces & legs
Piece under feet makes jigsaw complete
Quiet as a mouse under table playing house
Shake dice to GO for Snakes and Ladders or Ludo
String a cat's cradle making shapes if able
Taking fares on the bus on the stairs
Uncle Mac on the Radio, we sing as we go
Using boxes from shops for theatrical props

ROSEMARY SWIFT

70

Primary School Days

COLIN BALMER

My primary school, Shadow Moss, was an old three-room C of E church school in Moss Nook, Heald Green. Our education was provided by three ladies, Mrs. Goodwin, Mrs. Morrow and head mistress Mrs. Ashworth. The building was under the flight path to what was then, in the fifties, Ringway Airport. The traditional catchment area of the school had been rural Cheshire from local farms and lower middle class home owners with senior positions in the industry of south Manchester and the airport. Most of my contemporaries on the council estate of Woodhouse Park went to the local state school. However, my sister, brother and I were sent to Shadow Moss for an education with a solid Christian basis, prior to the Diocese of Shrewsbury catching up with the population migration from bombed-out slum dwellings in inner-city Manchester, by building the Catholic school of St Anthony's.

We working class kids from the council estate were in the minority. In general, I enjoyed school life, despite the outside toilets, absence of sports facilities and mixed-year classes. No identifiable class divisions came between post-war boys and girls – only the perennial gender partition. I was delighted to be taken to watch one of the first televisions in the area, at my best friend Richard's house. I don't recall sitting agog in front of the miniscule box, which needed delicate aerial adjustment. In the early fifties, I found much better entertainment in climbing trees, fishing for newts and chasing rabbits – treats unheard of for a peripatetic kid with previous homes with parents, uncles and grandparents in Ardwick and Bradford.

In the evenings, a different cohort of friends from the state school would congregate under the lamp post. Games and play were mostly divided along gender boundaries. The disparate squads of grazed knees and flashed knickers rarely united, which I guess contributed to my discomfort with the opposite sex – ironic as I look back over my life now.

The enlightened education system at Shadow Moss resulted in

Friday being allocated to the Arts. Dividing partitions were rolled back and the whole school was united in one assembly. Pupils would bring in their own selected books to exchange; we were led in singing, but the activity that really stood out was dancing. Unlike today's musical body popping we were taught disciplined dances like the waltz, tango and my dynamic favourite, the Polka. Although close contact with your partner (always the opposite sex – how quaint!) was mandatory, I never got anywhere near to a warm relationship. The one girl to whom I felt attraction, Christine, came from the Cheshire community and was, consequently, beyond my own self-conscious league.

The occasion that sticks strongest in my mind is the Christmas school play when I was about seven or eight. We were choreographed to enact the origin of the Order of the Garter in 1348. I suppose the teachers must have had an intention when appointing me as Henry III. As fate had it also, Christine had the role of Countess of Salisbury, who according to legend let her garter slip onto the dance floor at a court ball in Calais. In contempt for the sniggering courtiers, the king recovered the garter with the admonition *'Honi soit qui mal y pense'* – the catchphrase he was to use to drive his forces against the French. I was then scripted and urged to give the countess a kiss. This was too much for the shy, retiring and delicate youngster I was at the time. I don't remember struggling with the French slogan, but just could not face the shame and embarrassment of kissing a girl in public. The play and honour of being king stick proudly in my mind. I particularly remember the crown. Not one of those paper and sequins efforts – a genuine metal fabrication from brass plate that my Dad had made at work. It certainly weighed heavy on my young head. The shame of having to kiss a girl, however, expunged all subsequent memories of the play from my recall.

You will be pleased to hear, dear reader, that I subsequently conquered the stigma – but gloriously.

Sports Day

VERONICA SCOTTON

I only remember one sports day at. St Georges, though I'm sure I must have taken part in at least two.

When I joined the school, there was no girl's PE teacher, she had left before I started and was not replaced during the time that I went to that school. So, the RE teacher took her place. Mrs Riley had no enthusiasm for sport and basically supervised the girls changing into PE Kit, watched them haul out equipment and let us get on with whichever team sport was on the curriculum that day. If anyone didn't feel like taking part, the flimsiest excuse would be excepted so long as they didn't disrupt the ones that were taking part.

So when sports day came along, the Head of House teachers were fighting a losing battle to get volunteers to compete against each other on sports day. There were no qualifying levels of fitness or competence, just a willingness to take part was all that was needed.

At the same time there was a culture amongst the girls that it wasn't 'cool' to be good at sports and as hormones raced around pubescent bodies, it was more important to wear the shortest skirt, the longest eyelashes and be the one to supply the cigarettes (and other favours) behind the bike sheds.

I was new to the school, in fact new to the whole Secondary Modern culture. At St John's the boys and girls had been separated at the age of seven, so it was a novelty to share a classroom with the opposite sex. Being a late developer, I was only just beginning to understand the attraction of boys, I had 6 younger brothers, they were my equals, my friends.

I was also very competitive, so when the teacher came around asking for volunteers, my hand was the first to rise. Who will do the One hundred yards sprint? Me. Who can do Put Shot? Me! (

Whatever that is). Who can throw a javelin? Me, (how hard can that be, throwing a stick). I volunteered for every single sport including the swimming.

On the morning of the Sport's Day, volunteers were setting up the equipment, when a boy from my form, messing about, as boys do, ran the hurdles course, kicking down each hurdle on the way, to the cheers of his mates. When he came near me, I commented, 'But that's not clever, you would be disqualified if you knocked down the hurdle'. He answered 'No you don't, it doesn't matter if you knock them over, you just need to get to the finish line first'

I suppose I was probably quite fit. Trotting alongside the pram to school in Salford, keeping up with my mum's pace 4 times a day was probably good training. So as the starting gun fired, I set off running and didn't look back, the finishing line was the only thing in my sight and the ambition to win. I was the shortest girl in the lineup (I've never quite grown to 5 foot), but I came first.

I watched the boys throwing put shot and when it was my turn, didn't show myself up, I came second, the same with the javelin. But my starring moment was running the hurdles. Having no fear of knocking over the hurdles, I once again aimed for the finishing line, and did my best. I beat the Senior Girls Record. At the time I felt euphoric, my heart and head, swelled with pride, this was who I was, A winner. In hindsight, the school had only been open 4 or 5 years, not long enough to set high records, and a couple of years later twin girls from Malta took St Georges by storm and set the standards much higher.

The swimming gala came around and I came last in each event, I'd never perfected any stroke, my dad's lessons being cut short after the drowning incident. One embarrassing incident came in one race when a girl with the swimming club costume and hat touched the swimming line, followed soon after by the other competitors, while I had barely reached halfway with my doggy paddle (apparently it was OK not to be 'cool' in front of boys when swimming). Someone, one of the teachers I presume, drummed up encouragement for me and everyone in the pool started cheering me for my attempt. Come on Vaughan (my house), come on Williams, come Veronica. I could have died! This

74

wasn't me, I was a winner.

But at the end of the day, after marks were totted up, I won the coveted Victor Ludorum Trophy. Awarded to the competitor with the highest accumulated points. I stood on stage on my tiptoes as Phil Campbell, the winner for the boys, raised the trophy triumphantly. What a pair, he was probably nearly 6 foot and I was 4 foot 9 inches. He wore his designer trainers and I had market stall pumps, but none of that mattered, for once I had done well in sports and this was the thing my mum always boasted about. She would be proud of me.

The trophy with my name on it went into the cabinet in school and we received a small commemorative cup to take home. I still have the cup, The inscription on it is barely visible now. It is slightly battered and missing the base, it lived in my kids toy box for a few years, but it now stands on a shelf in my house, a reminder of the day when I was the best.

The Birthday Party

ALAN RICK

I suppose the children's birthday party is one of the earliest events that stay in the mind forever. These spectacles, organised as much for the parents themselves as for the children, made possible the display of the offspring in all their gaudy finery. It required the sort of lengthy and thorough preparation of the child that borders on the sadistic. The event I was dragooned into was the birthday of Janet, a little girl across the street. It seemed a slight enough cause to me considering the ordeal I was put through beforehand. This was to be scrubbed from head to foot, whiter than some peoples' doorsteps, to have my hair vandalised to reduce it to an acceptable length, to be decked out in clothes that I thought were only worn by dolls and to be on the receiving end of a moral lecture concerning manners, conduct and unattainable objectives. A small spirited boy was not meant for any of this I thought, as I glumly submitted to the strange preoccupations of the adult world. But perhaps the party itself would provide opportunities to sabotage it – we would see.

These parties followed a certain ritual – one shook the hand of Janet, with an air of feigned cordiality, and murmured a few words of courtesy, memorised from my mother's list drilled into me earlier that day.

The children, garbed as if at some exotic festival, were seated round a circular table eying the goodies, their eyes growing larger by the minute. Any attempt to touch any until the starting signal was firmly restrained by the parents, ranged like a circle of prison guards.

The parents had their own agenda in all of this, which was to secure two hours of peace and quiet while the children were engaged in the absorbing task of filling their faces.

Nowadays this would be achieved by the irritating means of the

76

Computer game. His or her room will be turned into a mass of wires and plugs and screens, the child will be wired up and plugged into about 40 controls worldwide and can spend the next two hours shouting at about three million children round the globe. Not in my day. At a party you just filled each child with about 3 times its weight in jelly, gave it a lump of play dough (then called Plasticine) and retired to put your feet up. Simple.

There was that wonderful moment during this party when Janet's mother, oozing maternal bliss from every pore, came round to each of us in turn with a large plate of cakes. At last, a reason for being here; grown-ups were not all wrath and finger wagging then and I had my fair share of greed. There were benefits in allowing the backs of your ears to be inspected and even your hair combed. At last the lady of the house approached me – this promised to be my lime-lit moment.

'And which cake would you like little Alan?' she gushed with a smile.

'The biggest.' I answered benignly.

My mother's face assumed the pallor of deep winter frost, the prison guards shifted uneasily and the laughter from the other children sounded like a gurgling drain.

Later that day at home the consequences were dire but not lasting. Would I try to sabotage adult morality again?

No – the price was too high and, in any case I would have to join them one day.

My Story of English

Stella M. Silverstein

I want to begin by saying, I had an unusual childhood, by most people's standards anyway. Most people are born in one country, live in that same country, and probably die in that same country. They might move to another city, or maybe move to one different country. This is a normal life for most people. My story is different.

I was born on an island off the coast of Southeast Asia (Philippines, 1974), my sister was born on a tiny island in the Pacific (Guam, 1978), and my brother on a tiny island in the Atlantic ocean (Bermuda, 1981). There are only the three of us. I was born in the same country as my mother, but my father was born in yet a different fourth country (USA). You see, my father was in the US Navy, and he had an adventurous soul. He didn't settle permanently in one place until I was about 15, when he finally retired from the military (1989). Funnily enough, he moved back home, back to the city where he was born before he started all his adventures. This is where I spent my teen years and early twenties. Now an adult, I live in a different (fifth) country (England, another island), but that is a story for another day.

I want to go back to my childhood; to the one place I had so many happy memories. Warm, breezy days full of sunshine, ocean adventures, and playing outside with my friends. We played kickball in the grass a few feet from my back door until our mothers called us in for dinner. I learned how to ride a bike on that grass, falling and getting green stains all over my clothes. I went roller skating outside underneath the carport. I would run inside the house when Sesame Street came on the only TV channel, and then run back outside when the show was over. I was a very dark brown child, always spending my days outside and only coming indoors for eating, sleeping, and attending school. I had a happy childhood.

I have very few memories of when I couldn't speak English very well, and I was mixing my words with two languages. My mother told me of a time when the school called her out of the blue and asked her to only speak English to me. I was speaking and mixing Tagalog (the official language of the Phillipines) and American English.

'We can't understand a word she says,' the school principal told her, 'She keeps mixing her English words with her other language. She doesn't speak a whole sentence in English.'

I was only very young at the time, maybe five, and just starting my first year of school. All my mother did was say OK, and I believe that was the day I started to gradually lose my first, my native, language.

As an adult I know now, my speech pattern gradually would have fixed itself naturally. I had the opportunity to grow up bilingual if my mother had disagreed with that school administrator. Two languages at home, with my mother speaking to me in Tagalog, my father speaking to me in English, and English instruction in school, I would be bilingual today, and the language mix-up fixed. This didn't happen. The day I started losing the ability to speak and comprehend my own native language, was the day the school called my mother and told her to teach me how to speak 'properly'. She only spoke to me in English from that day on. *Paalam Tagalog*, Goodbye Tagalog.

At that time, I was going to an American Department of Defense Dependents Schools (DoDDS). DoDDS are a network of primary and secondary schools all over the world, a very large school system that is based on the American curriculum. I was considered a 'military brat', and it's quite normal for brats to move to a different school and/or country on a pretty regular basis. We moved roughly every three years from the time I was a year old to the time I was fifteen. The schools try to allow a continuity of education in the same curriculum and school system, no matter what country a child is in.

My primary school principal called my mother that kindergarten day and told her to speak to me only in English. We were living in Guam at the time (1977-1980). They speak Chamorro in Guam. It is the goal for a DoDDS school to immerse the children attending the school in the local language and culture of the country where the school is. For example, the Kaiserslautern school in Germany teaches German language and culture to its students. In my Guamanian school, I was learning how to speak Chamorro, while at the same time I was told to improve my English language skills. I was forbidden to have my own native language spoken to me in order to improve my English. I guess it worked. I sound like a native American English speaker today as an adult, and everyone thinks that English is my native language.

I remember being six and learning Chamorro. That day in class we were learning the different words for girls and boys. In Tagalog girl is *babae* with each syllable pronounced and in Chamorro it's *palao`an*. Both languages have the same word for boy, which is *lalaki*. I remember this day quite well, and the teacher scolding me for trying to speak Tagalog.

By the time I was in the third grade, we moved to Bermuda (1980-1986) and, lucky for me at the time, Bermuda was a current English colony. Bermuda wouldn't get independence from the United Kingdom until 1995. We lived on an American naval base. In 1981 Bermuda became a British Dependent Territory as determined by the British government, changing its former status of a British crown colony, which meant I was now learning to speak British English along with my American English. I still spoke and understood Chamorro from Guam, and Tagalog (my native language) at the time.

While living in Bermuda I developed a love for the BBC World radio service, a love (which I still have) for English tea with milk,

80

thanks to my British neighbours and a love for English football. Thanks to my family, neighbours, primary school and my friends, my accent at the time was mixed. I heard American, English and Bermudian accents all throughout the day. These were some of the happiest years of my childhood, and I remember them very fondly. Bermuda was where my mother learned how to drive. We listened to the sounds of steel drums on the streets of Bermuda's capital, Hamilton. I learned how to swim at the beach just down the hill from the house and where I used to climb to the very top of the tree and sway in the wind. My mother's face turned almost white with fear one day when she caught me up a tree, swaying with the breeze. *Chingas* is the Bermudian word for surprise, and she sure was surprised to see me on a very thin tree in the Bermudian breezes.

I started winning spelling competitions in my third-grade year (1982-1983), attending another DoDDS school. I was writing and speaking English, although I'm not sure if I was using American or English spellings. My teachers were either Bermudian, English or American and I was hearing all three pronunciations. I had a huge desire to achieve and to please. I tried extra hard to be able to speak, read and write English to the best of my ability. In the fourth grade (1983-1984) I was placed in the Gifted and Talented Program (GATE). In the fifth grade I was placed in a mixed class of fifth and sixth graders due to my excellence in school. The school administration asked my parents if they wanted me to skip a grade and go straight into sixth grade. My parents declined. That was my last year in Bermuda, and that school. We moved to the USA for my last year of primary school, sixth grade (1985-1986).

We only spent one year in St. Louis, Missouri, USA. My father was born there and wanted to move his family 'back home'. He was going back to the USA after being gone for twenty plus years. This was my sixth-grade year, and I remember it vividly. We moved from sunny semi-tropical Bermuda to St. Louis in October. The leaves were changing colour and falling off the trees, the wind was starting to blow with a cold northern voice, and the smell of winter was already in the air. We had shorts, T-shirts and light jackets. My parents hastily got a loan, and bought us long trousers, long sleeved shirts, and thick winter jackets. We were still freezing that year, and I saw snow for the first time ever. I didn't even know it was cold and ran out without a jacket.

That one year in St. Louis changed my life linguistically. It was the first time when I was around 'normal' children and none of them were 'military brats' who moved to a different country every few years. These children and their siblings were born, lived and mostly died in the same area their parents did. Most of those same children still live there now as adults. The children at my school had no clue where Guam and Bermuda were, or even that they existed. They made fun of the way I talked, the way I was always cold, and how different my education was to theirs. I remember being constantly confused when they didn't understand something I said and I had to explain myself again and again.

My father was stationed on a ship in Virginia, away from us. My mother missed him and so did we. By the end of that school year, I finished primary school (1986) and my mother packed up all our stuff, put us all on a plane and we headed to Virginia, another state in the USA. That was the last year I remember speaking to my mother in my native language, Tagalog. I only spoke English after that year. I was determined that no one would make fun of the way I spoke again, and I would be understood. My accent became decidedly American. I was twelve at the time; an age where the great desire to fit in was just starting.

Recently I looked up that American base where I spent some of my happiest years on Bermuda. The base is now closed, the houses boarded up, and the streets are empty. The Bermudian government has taken over my school, and American children no longer attend there. I wanted to go back and visit, try to recapture some of that childhood warmth. *Mamiss*, I've noticed your absence in my life.

Toys and Outdoor Games

CHRIS MUTTON

Having recently celebrated my grandson's third birthday, and seen the thoughtful and varied presents he received despite the current lockdown, my thoughts turned to the toys of my childhood when money was scarce but my parents managed to regularly prove the adage 'poverty is the mother of invention'.

I grew up, in the fifties, in Little Hulton, when it was a small coal mining village and don't remember being aware that life was hard. All it took was a piece of string and my mother in a good mood and I was happy for hours playing cat's cradle with her. If her mood was really good she would use some of her precious donkey stone to draw the numbers for hopscotch on the main road pavement, at the front of our terraced house and, on occasion, even join in the game! The donkey stone was a bone of great contention to me. It was acquired from the rag and bone man in exchange for old clothes (those that hadn't been ripped up for dusters) but the alternative swap was a balloon which I really really wanted! I had no chance - my mother's maxim for judgement was, a) how white your 'whites' were and b) how clean your front path, including and especially how clean your doorstep was. Not only did your step have to be clean, it had to have a straight white edge - produced by the donkey stone. She also taught me how to play two balls against the kitchen wall and how to skip, including the very fancy French skipping -quite a different technique which necessitated the rope to be around the ankles of the two 'holders'. I also learned all the rhymes that went with these activities from her.

We were lucky to have a largish back garden in which we had a sand pit in an old sink and a nature table where we put our captured tadpoles and caterpillars in glass jars - the caterpillar jar holding lots of leaves. We had a swing in the coal shed doorway and woe betide us if we swung on the day the coal had been delivered and scattered it all over the yard. Many a happy summer day was spent in a tent made from an old army blanket thrown over the washing line, weighed down by as many old bricks as we could find. If it rained our tent was made indoors using the wooden maiden. Being an avid Enid Blyton reader a password was usually required to enter the tents and many an adventure was planned beneath the well-worn blanket.

My father was a great DIYer, not always successfully in the home – but, boy, could he knock together some great toys. My brother, Andrew, and I had walkie-talkies made from used bean cans and a piece of string, which we stretched between our bedroom windows for secret talks and messages. Dad also made us kites - which flew, spud guns from bits of wood and elastic bands and stilts from bean cans and pieces of string- these were a source of great envy amongst our friends until they too gained a pair, He also made us wooden ones but I mainly remember the splinters from the rough wood he used. Rough wood was also used to make us a 'bogie' - a handmade go-kart fashioned from a plank of wood, a bit of rope and wheels from an old pram. As children we didn't think to ask where he'd managed to get them from: as adults we think it probably better we don't know. A few years on, my brother proved he had inherited these skills when he made himself a skateboard - using MY roller skates (without permission I might add!)

As children it was always a good day for us when the washing line broke and had to be replaced and we gained a new skipping rope or lasso, although we quickly learned not to ask if the washing had been on the line when it snapped.

Many of our Christmas and birthday toys were made by our father. He used to get *The Hobbies Magazine* and kept each issue. Looking through these when sorting his possessions after he died was like taking a walk through our childhood, my brother's garage and fort; my doll's cot and a high chair; my double-fronted doll's house, with a front door that opened; a long wooden train with carriages and a large car transporter.

We didn't have a television for years because my father thought they would be the end of civilisation as we knew it - but we had a radio and parents who were always singing, my mum to herself, my dad to her. Not surprising then that my brother and I were both drawn to music. We learned how to play the spoons, and also the comb and my mother was not amused when father fashioned us a one string instrument out of her sweeping brush - and yes, the inevitable piece of string. We also got sore fingers from strumming the grill pan. But we thought our skiffle band was the best!

We had some bought toys - I think my best loved one was my doll's pram with my treasured dark skinned doll called Betty. Her arms and legs used to regularly fall off but my dad was always able to mend her with elastic bands and infinite patience, both skills I must be lacking because I am unable to fix her and so she lies, limbless, in a box in the loft. My friend Christine Ireland had a bigger doll's pram than me but didn't have a dark skinned doll so we frequently used to swap. My love for her pram was obviously greater than my love for my doll. However, we were always sent to swap back by our parents.

New toys were only given at Christmas, I can only remember a chalkboard, a desk and a toy tea set, which apparently led to the quietest Christmas my parents ever had as Andrew and I, concealed by mother's 'best' table cloth, played house under the table and drank sherry from the toy cups and then slept for the rest of the day.

Mostly I remember the books. We always got two annuals each - Andrew got *The Beano* and *Dandy* and mine were *Bunty* and *Schoolgirls' Friend*, but best of all I got an Enid Blyton book every year, from either *The Famous Five*, *Secret Seven* or *Adventure* series. Our uncle in Australia also sent us books every year and, to my disgust, I always got a *Rupert Bear* annual - I was told to be grateful but actually, I was envious of Andrew who always got the adventure ones such as *The Walkabout Plot*, *The Railway Children*, *Robin Hood* - little surprise that I used to think that 'boys books' were better than 'girls'. The other much-looked-forward-to present, this time in my stocking, was a tin of *Holland's Caramels*, which had a different picture on the front every year,- not only for the sweets but for the picture on the lid, sometimes flowers, other times Scottie dogs or kittens. Having eaten the sweets, the tin was used as a crayon box for the rest of the year. In the stocking, along with the toffees, was a tangerine, an apple and a shiny new penny to be kept until New Year's Eve when it was put under my pillow to ensure I would never be without money through the next year.

We played out a lot, either in a 'gang' or just my friend **Christine and I making perfume from rose petals or playing with our cut out dolls bought from Hennan's book stall on Farnworth Market or from the back of our weekly comic, *Bunty*. If we were lucky her dad, Uncle Ted, would make us a see-saw from his garden roller and his decorating plank.

Another favourite activity was to go to The Co-op Bakehouse, which was just off the A6, before Clegg's Lane, to see the cart horse in its stable - and shamefully, to help ourselves to the vanilla cream left in plastic buckets near the large wooden doors - no wonder we were regularly chased away by an irate Mr Crompton!

Bike riding was always done in summer - the trend being to put an ice lolly stick in between the spokes of the wheel to make it sound like a motorbike. Often bikes were inherited and something to 'grow into' No problem was unsolvable in those days and if the bike was too big and pedals couldn't be reached, blocks were made over the pedals. Picnics, with the obligatory jam butty and bottle of water were held in our dens made from debris found on the bankings and materials begged, borrowed or stolen from Dad's or Uncle Ted's garden sheds. However, the bankings weren't only seen as a source of foraging. One of our favourite games was to slide down the banking on an old piece of lino or in a cardboard box (easier to hold onto but not as long-wearing as the lino) - usually waiting for the train to be coming before we set off! Other sources for our dangerous activities were stairwells - sliding down them on old trays or, as we got older, jumping down them, increasing the number of steps each time we jumped.

We also played 'dares' and my heart still goes into my mouth when I remember one of these and my brother walking across the railway bridge on Mount Skip Lane- along the edge of the parapet!

On one side of this very wide lane were new houses, on the other a large field where the Co-op horses grazed, alongside the geese and chickens who had their pens there. The only accidents I can remember were: when our friend Martin got his head stuck in the railings and, on a separate occasion, his brother, Michael, got his foot stuck and was attacked by the geese. These antics never went unpunished because despite there not being any phones, when we got home, all our parents knew where we had been and early bed without supper was imposed. I'm sure the ever present danger of the railway track was the reason this was forbidden territory because, in summer, we were allowed to walk through Bluebell Woods (now the huge Madam's Wood Estate) to Mosley Common and a strange little place called City, which consisted of just a row of terraced houses and a post box. Independence that we probably wouldn't be allowed these days.

Discussing these memories before putting them into words has made my brother, friend and myself laugh, a lot. We certainly hadn't realised quite how 'feral' we were as children. Whilst I wonder how surprising it is that I don't remember many of the bought toys, but can rattle off the made and invented ones, there's no question that what IS surprising is that we all survived to tell the tales!

**My friend Christine wanted me to include the homemade salad cream with marmalade sandwich we used to make and eat. We called them Christine Specials. I couldn't quite fit them into a relevant paragraph - maybe next time!

Childhood holidays

PAUL HALLOWS

Every year since I was six years old, my mum organised a holiday for disabled people and their carers to Weston Super Mare once a year in October .

There were about fifty of us and we travelled by a special coach which had a lift on it and a hoist for the people who couldn't transfer to their seat.

We always went to Pontins holiday camp in Sand Bay. We met up with up to four hundred of our friends. They were from similar groups from Walsall, Halesowen, Black Country, Birmingham, Rowley Regis and many more.

We stayed for a week. It was great. Cabaret and bingo every night and various activities during the day. All sorts going on.

My dad wasn't into bingo, so I would get him a coffee from the cafe and he would get the chance for a smoke.

Sunday was always the ramble, Wednesday the fancy dress which was the highlight of the week. Nearly everyone took part. There was a choice to go to the shops around Weston town centre in the afternoon if you wanted to. Friday was red, white and blue night .There was also wrestling and table tennis on.

I was always picked as the ball boy when the table tennis was on. There were two professional players and every time they knocked the ball off the table I had to pick it up and give it back to them. Every so often, they would use about ten balls at a time, which they would knock off. Of course, I had to pick them up. When I got back to the table I tried to put them back on. As I had all ten in my hand they would just bounce off everywhere - to lots of laughter from the audience. As you can tell this went on for some time.

There was a swimming pool on site as well. So we used to take some of the crowd with us. Really the campsite was just for adults but, because it was a special week, they let children go as well. One of the Bluecoats, Katie, had all the kids playing games and things. We had a swimming race which I won and I got a medal for it which I was chuffed about.

They had a games room where we could play snooker, bowls and much more. It was a great holiday. Everyone loved it.

Unhinged

CHRIS VICKERS

When I was a kid Dad was the ultimate threat regarding misbehaviour, as in: 'just you wait until your Dad gets home!' On a hook near the cellar door hung the 'nuclear option' a leather strap that was to be wielded by him in the event of any newsworthy infractions. He was, however, despite a gruff exterior, a mild and easy-going fellow who longed for a quiet life. The nuclear option was never invoked.

Mum on the other hand was a small, wiry, high-energy individual who really ran the show and was possessed of a fiery temperament. Her temper was probably genetically linked to her brother's bright red curly hair. My lineage was definitely from the distaff side as I was totally unlike my quiet, studious siblings. All my young life endless 'jokes' about the milkman persisted.

I was full of devilment which I would normally curtail by ceaseless physical activity but I remember on one occasion being stuck at home with no mates around to interact with. In such times poor Mum would become targeted and pestered and driven to distraction. Eventually and after endless warnings, she would give me such a scutch leaving red and ringing lugholes. On this particular day I managed to put in an Olympic gold performance though, needling her to such an extent that 'the dam finally broke'. She had the 'red mist' and I'd pushed her too far, like when the eyes of the matador and bull meet and each knows they've reached the point of no return. I turned on my heels and flew through the sitting room from the kitchen and mounted the stairs two at a time, hotly pursued by an incandescent mother: diving through my bedroom door and wedging my foot at the bottom, just before she hurled her infuriated body at it. A horrific rending sound ensued as the door split from the top down to the hinge. A moment's silence.

'Bloody hell,' I thought.

'Bloody hell,' Mum exclaimed.

I sheepishly opened the door.

'We'd better not tell your Dad,' she said and I nodded.

As ever our furies were spent and forgotten, never to be thought of again, still less spoken about and instead of being antagonists we were again united, complicit in hiding our indiscretions from Dad and his nuclear option.

Veronica Scotton – Life's Lessons

I remember playing 'house' in the bombed ruins of buildings. Everything needed to enact our imaginations, lay at our feet. Broken bricks and planks of wood, arranged to create rooms, chairs or tables. Roof tiles for plates and mud for food.

Sometimes we had real dolls to be our babies, sometimes we had real babies, if we had the use of one. It was quite normal for little girls to knock on doors and ask

'Can I take your baby for a walk?'

And completely acceptable for a busy housewife to let a child walk off, pushing a pram containing their precious offspring, with the instruction to:

'Bring him back for his 2 o'clock feed'

Having younger siblings had its advantages, on the days they could be persuaded to co-operate.

Working class housewives didn't have coffee mornings, but the kettle was always on, simmering until the next neighbour dropped in for a brew and a fag. Children were sent out to play, seen but not heard.

One summer, on one of these occasions, we made a den by throwing a blanket over four kitchen chairs and played doctors and nurses, with pretend bandages and plasters and sugared water for medicine. It was also the excuse to examine bits of body that wouldn't normally be on show,' like doctors do'. My seven year old conscience had reservations about this, a teacher at school had once told us that your conscience was like having your mother watching you. If you were doing something that you wouldn't want your mam to watch, then it was probably a sin. The following Saturday I presented myself in the confessional, 'Bless me Father, for I have sinned, it is one week since my last confession.' I

92

continued, telling in detail of our childish games, secretly hoping that Father O'Reilly would tell me that it wasn't a sin and so give me permission. Of course he didn't, he told me to say one Our Father, two Hail Mary's and *'never to do that again.'* So when the next opportunity presented itself, I had to sit it out and watch. The other children partaking were only five or six years old, so not capable of sinning yet.

My present from my granny Williams one Christmas, was a packet of Liquorice Allsorts.

I handed it back saying, 'No thanks granny, I don't like liquorice.'

After she had gone, I was reprimanded and told that I should have thanked her and given them away later. There have been changes in etiquette since then, I would rather my grandchildren put me straight, rather than me going on presenting them with sweets they didn't like.

Another year, Father Christmas brought me a pair of roller skates, but I was only allowed to wear one at a time, in case I fell over, therefore I got far more pleasure from my brothers' Lego. The same year, my best friend Stella, received a pair of glass slippers with a little heel, my mam worried about her breaking her ankle, tried to persuade her to wear just one at a time too.

Once, I absentmindedly put half a crayon in my cardigan pocket at school. When my mam came across it, she took me back into school to apologise. As I stood in front of the class the teacher pointed out to the class, the thief in their midst. She said I wouldn't be punished on this occasion, but there were no second chances. I was five years old!

I couple of years later, now in the Juniors, I returned to school after having a couple of days off. We had new desks that we had to polish each Friday afternoon. Someone had drawn a zigzag with an eraser in the polish. Miss Kelagher, the teacher called me to the front of the class to explain why I had defaced the desk. I protested that it wasn't me, but her reply was that I was a liar,

'Who else would write the initials V W'

93

This time I got the ruler across the palms of my hands. I was so upset, not just because of the punishment, but because she had called me a liar. When my mum came to pick me up from school, she of course wanted to know why I was upset and hearing the story, led me back into the classroom. She was not a shy retiring kind of woman, and was going to 'sort this teacher out'. But when she came face to face with her old teacher from St Joseph's, her whole demeanour changed. She had been her bully of a teacher 20 years before. We walked home without ever discussing the incident again.

In spite of the bullying regime, I liked school and was quite a good scholar, but when asked how I thought I had done in the eleven plus exam, I said that I had not understood some of the sums because I didn't know what the dots were for. (I had never been introduced to decimals). When the results were published and I had failed, I was disappointed and so were my parents.

My mum remarked, ' I wouldn't have expected Lorraine to have passed.'

I told her that the ones that had passed were the ones that had stayed later at school for extra tutoring. She went into school for an explanation and was told that the girls with the most potential had been coached. She pointed out that I had always been in the first or second place each year.

'Yes,' agreed Mother Bernadette, 'but we didn't think you would be in a position to afford the uniform.'

In the eyes of this middle class nun, I was not Adelphi House material.

There was always a silver lining. On the run up to the eleven plus, my mum had bribed me with a typewriter or a doll if I passed. But one day she slipped up and said bike (I think this slip was caused because my younger cousin had just got a bike, and she liked to keep up with the Jones') not surprisingly I answered 'bike'. Afterwards my dad insisted that I received the bike because of the way that I had been cheated. I thought all my birthdays and Christmases had come together when choosing the yellow and turquoise bike with the modern straight handlebars from Leonards of Salford,. It was my pride and joy for years. But in hindsight, my brothers got far more fun from it than I did. Because it was impressed upon me how lucky I was to have this expensive gift, I was always very cautious not to damage it and spent every weekend, polishing it to keep it in tip top condition. Once I grew out of it, my brothers got it as a second hand bike and needed no such caution. They crashed it up and down the bankings, made ramps and race tracks. They were even caught at one time lighting a fire with the intention of doing an Evil Knievel.

My mam taught us to knit and to juggle two balls, (one, two, three alera), to do handstands against the wall, tucking her skirt into her knicker leg. She demonstrated how to skip with a rope and all the chants that went with it. On days spent at Peel Park, she demonstrated how to roll down the hill, and told us about the time she had split her head open, as a child doing it. My dad knocked the top and bottom from a wooden box and screwed it to the wall as a netball net.

A month after my 10th birthday, my brother Perry was born. My mam never made any concessions to her condition and carried on with all the hard manual labour that was housework in the 60s. But she got a wake up call when, towards the end of the pregnancy, she was warned that the baby was in distress and she had to be taken into hospital to be induced. When the ambulance bringing her home stopped outside our house, it was like an antennae to all the kids from around the streets. They crowded around the ambulance asking:

'Is it the nit nurse?'

Before the end of the week, she was in full swing, no convalescing for her. One bright June day, when Perry was still only a couple of weeks old she got up, fed him, top and tailed him and popped him into the pram outside the front door. She then sorted out the rest of her 6 kids and walked the one and a half miles, to drop us eldest 3 at school, then back home with youngest. As Perry was still sleeping peacefully, she left him in the pram outside the front door, made a brew and then, completely out of character, she fell asleep on the settee with Gail snuggled up next to her and Gary playing innocently in front of the unlit fire.

Well it was a tiny two-up, two-down terraced house, with the minimum of storage. In the kitchen the one small cupboard held cleaning and cooking stuff, the sideboard in the front room held everything else. This must have presented itself to three year old Gary, as Aladdin's cave. At first he emptied all the food from out of the cupboard, covering himself and the floor with sugar and tea leaves. Next he lifted out the iron and plugged it in. At some point he found scissors and decided to give Gail a haircut, she never felt a thing and she never forgave him.

When Perry woke up and loudly announced his hunger, mam woke up and wondered why she was covered in blond hair, then startled to see and smell, black smoke pouring out from under the iron, which by this time, was welded to the smouldering lino.

We will never know how she handled the situation, it perhaps included lots of shouting and slaps, or more likely crying and thanking God that Gary hadn't hurt himself or burnt the house down. Recriminations to herself, for not being a perfect mother. Nevertheless, by noon, the mess had been cleared away, Gail's hair had been trimmed to match the other side, Perry had been fed, the dinner organised and mam stood outside school waiting for the doors to open. She related the story of her morning to other mothers in the school yard and then she repeated the tale hundreds of times over the years. It always began with 'Did I ever tell you what that little bugger did once'

Gary craved attention and praise, but unfortunately that was not the way of the northern, working class family during the 50s. Parents didn't want offspring growing up soft, or with ideas above their station. He brought a little girl home from school once and told her 'Tell me mam who's the best in our class'

She answered shyly 'You are Gary.'

He said 'right you can go home now.'

Whenever any of us came home hoping for praise for an achievement:

'I got the Victor Laudorum.' 'I came top in maths.' ' I've been made a prefect' 'I've got a solo part in the play' etc It would be

Top Trumped by our mother with a higher achievement of another sibling who wasn't present (she wouldn't boast about you within your hearing)

Most housewives of the time, scrubbed the street in front of the house with a scrubbing brush and a donkey stone, (A scouring block used in the North of England to highlight the edge of stone steps). Because Stella's mam was older and frail the job fell to Stella. But also, in the past Mrs Barratt, had taken on the task of doing the doorsteps of two elderly neighbours and so Stella inherited those too. So at 8 years old she took over three door steps and pavements right down to the kerb. By the time she was eleven years old, her mother had died and so she was expected, as the only girl in the house, to take over the rest of the housework and run around after her dad and two brothers.

Perhaps Mrs Barratt knew she was dying, because early in the year Stella and Stephen, her brother, had a joint birthday party and I was invited. Two cakes, one pink, one blue. Jelly and ice cream, paste butties, pass the parcel. My eyes were opened, I had never experienced anything like it. They also had a telly that on occasion I was invited in to watch. Cheyenne Bodie on a Saturday afternoon. The height of poshness.

Each week, my dad took me to the library where I was only allowed to take one book. Adults were allowed four and so in the time he took to choose, I would read one book before choosing another one to take home. He taught me to swim at Regent Road Baths. On one occasion taking five of us, Gary aged four, Gail five, Ian seven, Kevin eight and me ten. They didn't have showers, that I can remember, but a big concrete trough of warm water at the side of the swimming pool, in which we all loved to sit, and had to be persuaded to leave. When it was time to go home, my dad decided to swim one length by himself and told us to sit against the wall at the shallow end to wait for him. As he prepared to dive in at the deep end, Gary shouted 'catch me dad' and jumped in. My dad had never swum a length so fast in his life. Gary often used to catch his breath when frightened or shocked and did so on this occasion. The life guard pulled him out as his eyes rolled to the back of his head and started to do CPR, whilst I shouted:

'That's my brother, leave him alone.'

When we got home and regaled my mam with the story, she banned Dad from ever taking us swimming again and so my youngest three brothers didn't learn to swim until they went swimming with the school.

Each year at school, a fancy dress dance was held, with prizes for the most imaginative costumes. Being a 'girls only' school, most costumes consisted of fairies, queens or ballet dancers. My dad had other ideas. There was a National campaign at the time to reduce the number of children being killed on the roads and he took his inspiration from this. I wore a white dress with black horizontal stripes, I was a zebra crossing. In my hand I carried a Belisha beacon, a black and white striped pole, with an orange crepe paper globe on the top. He had fitted a battery to the bottom of the pole so that each time I placed it on the ground, the beacon lit up.

I was mortified, and tried, without success to make my dad understand that I would be laughed at for the rest of my school life. But I won first prize and I was the girl everyone wanted to talk to the next day, thanks to my clever dad. The next year, I went in a dress, with paper flames and a fireguard, the theme being Fire Safety, The idea coming from the crusade to reduce the number of children dying, or being maimed by fire, especially fireworks. I won every year until the year that Stella's mum died and my dad dressed us both. She went as the Bow Bells of London and won, and I went as Lidiya Pavlovna Skoblikova, the Russian olympic ice skater. Selfishly I was secretly miffed that she had won instead of me. How spoiled was I, she had won a prize but had come to the end of her childhood.

I don't hanker after my childhood. I think my kids and grandchildren are very lucky to have the opportunities and technology that they have. I love the fact that I can pick up my phone and the contact details of everyone I know are in my hand. I love that I can communicate with people in other countries with the help of the translate technology. But my childhood helped to shape the person I am, I have never felt the need to have more money, a bigger house or a faster car and never suffered from mental health issues. So I count my blessings, enjoy the life I have and look forward with optimism to the future.

SQUIRES GATE 1959

Apart from days out to Bellevue, Heaton Park and Blackpool, the only holiday we had as a family was a week at Squires Gate, the station before Blackpool on the train.

The excitement of a holiday! 'What's a holiday mam?' All our clothes for a week for Mam, Dad and five children were packed into two suitcases, which my dad carried for the half an hour walk to catch the train. The youngest of us was Gary, snug in his pram, and Gail a year older sat at the other end with a warning from my mam to 'watch you don't kick the baby' The tray underneath the pram was filled with Terry nappies and groceries, a flask of tea and sweets for the journey. We had new clothes, bought on Cross Lane Market and my very thrifty mam had got a selection of knitted clothes from a jumble sale, unravelled the wool and washed it to straighten it and then twisted two colours of wool together and knitted them up once more into new cardigans for each of us. I was always happy to get a new jumper and would tell the world the whole story of its creation. My mam's sister, my Auntie Margaret, who liked to think she was a class above, would advise me 'If anyone asks where you got your clothes from, say Marks and Spencer.'

Our house was on Muslinet Street, which was next to Cow Lane, where animals were off-loaded from the railway siding to take their last walk to the Cattle Market and the abattoir. Therefore the smell and noises of trains was not new, but we had never been to Victoria Train Station in Manchester before, never heard the cries of 'All Aboard'. The piercing screech of the whistle, and the noise of the huge engine as it pulled into the station frightened Gary so much he screamed and wouldn't be consoled. Mam was stressed, she had been up early to get us ready, ever the worrier, she imagined every eventuality that could possibly happen. What if she lost one of us, what if we got sick?, What if the train crashed? Boarding the train brought back terrifying childhood memories of being packed onto a train with her younger brother and sister, each with a gas mask as they were evacuated to Lancaster during the war. Dad took everything in his stride, helping us to get washed and dressed, making breakfast, filling the flask, refereeing squabbles, locking the cases.

My heart was racing as we boarded the train and settled down with library books colouring books and crayons, and a packet of cards for playing Snap. The train pulled out of the station and we left the sooty streets of Salford behind, we whizzed past farmers' fields and little villages and stopped at stations to pick up more passengers as we went. What an adventure!

 We stayed in a converted train carriage which had a gang plank to walk across to get to the field next to it. There was a sand pit on the field, the only amenity included, and there were gas lamps to light the carriages in the evening although I don't remember any heating, however, caravans at the time had coal fires, so maybe that did too.

My dad's teenage cousin, Doreen, came with us to babysit, so that mam and dad could go out in the evening but they never did, but she was an extra pair of hands during the day and my most lucid memory of this time was her trying to teach me to whistle. I would watch carefully while she pursed her lips and blew, then I would try, but the act of pursing my lips made me giggle and you can't purse your lips and laugh at the same time. My giggles were infectious and dad's voice would call out, 'What are you two finding so funny out there?' One rainy day, Kevin and Ian, routing

100

through the carriage found Mam's corset and climbed into it. They emerged like co-joined twins except Kevin had white blond straight hair and Ian's hair was wavy dark brown. Mam tried to be cross at them messing with her stuff, but couldn't stop laughing and the rest of us were convulsed

We children were happy to play on the field with other children as they appeared from other carriages, my five year old brother Ian fell in love with a little girl 'covered in blonde hair' he couldn't wait to get out each morning to see if she was there and then he would follow her all day and hang on to her every word.

Gail was not a happy child about this holiday, each morning she would be traumatised to find she was still not in her own bed at home and would ask 'Why are we still here, when are we going home?'

One day we walked to the Pleasure-Beach in Blackpool where Doreen and Dad took us on the rides, Mam stayed with the babies and the pram, minding the coats, smoking and drinking tea from the flask. We had candy floss and Blackpool Rock and bought souvenirs to take home to our grans, we laughed at the Laughing Policeman, watched Punch and Judy on the beach and had a donkey ride.

Other days we would walk to the nearest beach with our buckets and spades and bats and balls. We built castles with moats and decorated them with seagull feathers and sea shells, then paddled in the sea and dried ourselves with sandy towels. I learned to cartwheel and listened to mam's stories about how when she was a girl she could do backflips. I've never learned how to backflip. Bottles of pop or water to drink and jam butties to eat were carried to the beach under the pram and in the late afternoon, all our paraphernalia was loaded up for the walk home for tea. We wore sun hats sometimes but no mention was ever made of sunscreen. On one such occasion, Gail sat on a giant jelly fish and screamed at the top of her voice. Dad remarked 'that girl's got some lungs on her' and strolled over to pick her up. 'Come on, luv' it's only a jelly fish' But she continued to scream hysterically. Shouting, 'My bum's hurting'. He looked and was shocked to see huge blisters appearing all over her bottom and legs. Leaving the rest of us on the beach with Doreen, mam and dad ran into town, carrying their still screaming daughter. They ran into a chemist to ask for something to sooth the burns. On hearing the story and seeing the blisters, the chemist directed them to a doctor's surgery. The doctor took one look and out of his cupboard brought a tube of cream with 'foreign' writing on. He said that it was very lucky that they had come to him because he could see by the injury that this jelly fish was a long way from home and was usually only found in warmer waters. The only reason he knew about it and had the cream handy, was that the year before he had been to Spain, where his daughter had done the same thing as Gail. The cream was administered, the tears subsided and we had fish and chips in a cafe because it was way past our tea time.

The week came to an end, as all weeks do. Doreen gave Gary his bottle while Mam packed the suit cases and reminded us to 'Have a wee before we go' she was glad the week was over, 'I'll never do this again, too much bloody trouble!' she exclaimed! Dad looked under each bed to make sure nothing was left behind, then took us out for a walk to get us out from under everyone's feet. Ian said a sad goodbye to his little girlfriend.

Being sad to go meant I was not in the mood for laughter and I eventually managed to whistle.

Gail cried, she didn't want to go home.

RESPONSIBILITY

Although, I seem to remember walking to and from school each day firmly holding onto the Silver Cross pram, or as the family grew, walking close by, there were occasions when we were trusted to make the journey unsupervised.

On one occasion, two of my brothers and I made the journey by ourselves with me, being the eldest in charge in theory. With mam's warnings ringing in our ears of 'mind the road' and 'don't dawdle' we turned right out of our front door along our street, turned left onto to Muslin street and right again onto Cow Lane where we met up with my friend and her brother,who always made the journey alone. So far so good, these were only quiet minor roads.

As we reached Oldfield Road, often referred to as 'the dock road' the traffic was busy and other pedestrians were bustling along to catch a bus, go to work or, like us, head towards St Johns Cathedral School. We passed over the railway bridge and passed the Victorian Dwellings. As we got to the end of The Dwellings we stopped at the crossing where a very jolly Lollipop Man stopped the traffic so that we could cross safely. We knew the drill and waited patiently until he shouted us to cross and then set off en masse on his command of 'come on you lot'. By this time I was in the middle of a gossip with my friend and no longer had hold of Ian's hand. He ran across the main road, but then didn't stop and turned left without looking and carried on across the minor road leading on to it, where he was knocked down by an Austin Mini Countryman. I was going to 'Get Done'

My heart stopped, the driver and his passenger jumped out of the car, a small crowd gathered around. They had not been speeding and Ian wasn't dead but just as I thought we could carry on with our journey to school, already planning how I could keep this calamity from reaching my Mam's ears, the couple lifted him into their car and said they would take him to Salford Royal to get him checked out. What was I supposed to do? I got hold of Kevin's hand (closing the stable door after the horse had bolted), he was as shocked as I was and anyway far too sensible to run into the road and we continued to school.

On reaching school I tried to tell Miss Jones about the accident, but couldn't make myself heard as other more assertive voices grabbed her attention and then it was time for assembly and prayers. It wasn't until the lesson proper had started that I dared to put up my hand to speak. 'Yes Veronica, I hope this is important' 'Yes Miss, it is!' 'Well go on then' 'Our Ian's bin knocked down' This got her attention and that of the whole class, 30 little girls had just heard some news that might keep the teacher's attention long enough for her to forget about the spelling test. Miss Jones' voice became more kindly and that was my undoing, my chin began to wobble, tears welled up in my eyes and the built up stress of the morning made the recount of the accident much more dramatic. She sent me to the Headmistress of the Junior department, Mother Bernadette, where I retold the story. She sent me down to the Infants to speak to Sister Theresa and by the time she had passed me on to Ian's teacher, my rendition of the story deserved an Oscar. It was decided that the teacher from the nursery class would take me in her car (what excitement, there's a first time for everything) to Salford Royal to find out if my brother was OK.

Ian was in his element, with his brown curls, and beautiful eyes he had won the heart of the nurses. He was eating biscuits and drinking milk while the medical staff wondered what to do with him. The couple who had taken him in had declined all responsibility as soon as it was apparent that he had no injuries and Ian couldn't remember his address. Of all of us, Ian was the one with the imagination, so God alone knows what his rendition of the accident was.

The teacher drove us home, even though I implored her to take us back to school, there was no way I would get away with this now, but when we got home our Mam had gone out. The door was never locked so we went inside, but the teacher would not leave us there alone and asked if we knew any of the neighbours.

Several of our neighbours were the older, respectable kind of people who cleaned their windows and washed the nets every week, some even had televisions. We didn't choose any of those, we chose the Jolly's who lived straight across the street from us. Mr and Mrs Jolly and their children Julie and Jimmy were lovely, 'give you their last h'penny' kind of people, but they were not the most house proud.

Meanwhile, Mam had arrived at school to pick up her three children and found only one. She was reassured that her other two children were safely waiting with a neighbour. Kevin, unsure what part of the incident would be likely to upset the most, just said he couldn't remember.

By the time Mam got home and we tripped across the road in trepidation to tell her the events of the morning, the whole of

Salford knew about poor little Ian. We needn't have worried, she was so embarrassed that the teacher had gone into the least salubrious house in the street, she forgot to be mad at me for letting go of his hand.

I can't for the life of me recall Kevin's reactions during this time. The poor little boy must have been sitting behind his desk not knowing whether his brother was lying in a hospital bed or been kidnapped by the couple in the car. He had no way of knowing whether he would be blamed alongside me for not keeping Ian safe and therefore have to suffer Mams wrath or even worse our Dad's. But 60 years later he doesn't even remember the incident so all's well, that ends well.

THE OLD VIC

Everyone remembers what they were doing, so it is said, when they heard about the death of JFK, the heartthrob President of America.

I was in the middle of doing a 'crab' which was to be part of a routine at my dancing class, a chilly room above a pub, on Oldfield Road, in Salford. Clare Bennet, the teacher was supporting my back and telling me to kick my legs over and stand up ready for the next bit of the dance. In theory it was a tap and ballet class and I vaguely remember learning the first five ballet poses, but mostly we learned different routines to sing and dance to. I probably only attended a year at most, before our 'flit' to Little Hulton with the slum clearances.

Back to the drama of JFK.

Someone dashed into the room hysterically screaming 'John Kennedy has been shot!' The hand supporting my back disappeared and I landed in a heap. The dancing was forgotten, some of the women sitting around the room, waiting for their daughters, began to cry. They tried to tune the radio in to a news station to find out if it was true.

By the next week as the class came around, it was back to

business. Two or three times a year, the class would put on amateur shows for pensioners. Little girls singing and dancing to lift the spirits of working class people, in post war Salford. I remember singing and dancing to:

'Joshua, Joshua, Sweeter than Lemon Squash you are!'

And *'The Sun is as High as an Elephant's eye'*

I remember the costume I wore to perform 'Joshua' was a black coat with tails, a top hat and a walking cane. As I sang my heart out, head held high, smiling at my audience, I didn't know then, that I have the singing voice of a frog, I've never been able to hold a note, Too late now to apologise to all those poor old dears that came along to be entertained. They were probably thinking 'Aw Bless, she's doing her best', or maybe 'Get her Off!'

One day as I signed into the class, the teacher asked me my age and was delighted that I was just turned 12. They had been approached by a professional group to supply a number of girls to join the chorus line for a pantomime. It was Aladdin And His Wonderful Lamp, and it was to be performed at the Victoria Theatre (The Old Vic), in Salford. I'm not sure of the reason why my age was important, something about how many hours children were allowed to work. Being small for my age I could act the part of a younger child. She asked me if I had any friends who were about my size and so I recruited my best friend Stella.

The dance class supplied two groups of girls if memory serves. A younger group and some taller ones. Stella and I managed to perform in nearly every scene as, for whatever reason, we would be dressed in one costume and dance with the younger ones and then quickly change costume to go on again with the big ones. As I say, I don't know the reason, children in those days were talked at, more often than being asked their opinions. The older girls got £2 10s a week and us younger ones £1 10 shillings. I think Stella and I might have been given a couple of shillings more because we danced more than all the rest of the troop.

For one scene we had to wear black ballet shoes and the theatre didn't provide them so my mum had to buy some. I only wore them once and managed to lose one on the way home. She couldn't afford another pair and so went to the market and bought a pair of black pumps and I had to make do.

For one scene, all of the girls were dressed as exotic birds with luminous costumes, I remember that they came out of the prop room and smelled of mustiness and sweat. Being the smallest two, during one act, we had to forward-roll across the stage. I starting from one side and Stella from the other. We had hoods on with beaks attached to the front which made tippling over a bit tricky and by half way we were both slightly dizzy.

On the evening performance when my parents and siblings came to watch the show, I was a bit nervous to get it right, which automatically ensured that I would do something wrong. As I knelt behind the curtain waiting for my cue, I caught sight of my family and waved frantically at them. Of course half the audience spotted me and started laughing and my dad was making shooing movements with his hands, to tell me to get back behind the curtain. The whole scene was performed in pitch black so that only the luminous bird costumes could be seen. Because I hadn't been paying enough attention I missed the cue and when I looked up it was to see that Stella had started to roll. Panicking I started my forward rolling, going a bit quicker, hoping that no-one had noticed my late start. But it wasn't to be. The audience, who had already seen the little bird waving from the side, now watched as it tippled a little too quickly across the stage. Embarrassed I didn't notice when I got to the part where I should have passed by Stella, and instead crashed into her and then overbalanced and fell into the orchestra pit.

The only thing hurt was my pride, perhaps the audience thought it was part of the show.

On the last day of the performances the cast had a party. It comprised of plenty of food and drink, singing and talking. We were allowed to join in if we got permission. The only person I knew at that time who possessed a phone was a friend who's parents ran a pub. I was allowed to use the theatre phone. I phoned Lyn, who ran around to my house to ask for permission. At the end of the last performance, my dad came to chaperone us, having gone round to inform Stella's dad that he would keep an eye on her and bring her home later.

It was a magical experience, all the lights in the theatre were turned off, the seats covered in white dust sheets, just a few lamps to light up the stage where the party was being held. Someone had a guitar and soon songs, that always seemed to get sung by a crowd, were sung:

There was rats, rats, as big as bloody cats

In the Store, In the Store,

There was Rats, Rats, as big as Bloody cats

In the Quartermaster Store

My Eyes are Dim, I Cannot See

I Have Not Brought My Specs with Meeee....

Getting rowdier and ruder as the alcohol was consumed. As soon as they ran out of versus for one song, another would begin. I remember my dad toning it down, when it got to his turn, by singing

'I know a girl and her name was Stella,

hey lardy, lardy low,

She couldn't shout, but she could Bella, hay lardy, lardy low.

Of course the next person had to think of a name who's rhyme had smuttier connotations

Stories were told of the White Lady. Every good theatre should have one, and each actor had a favourite story that, 'Hand on Heart was the God's truth'.

At some point we decided to creep away from the lighted stage and crept into the auditorium to investigate what it was like in the Royal Box. It was too tempting, when we got there, not to act the fool. I climbed onto Stella's shoulders and pulled the dust sheet over my head and started howling in the way that I was sure a good ghost would. A few drunken actors started screaming, others laughed, until my dad's voice rang out. 'Get down you two, before you fall out of there and break your necks'

As it got to midnight, someone went out and brought back meat and potato pies. The atmosphere had quietened we children way past our bedtimes. I had just dragged my sleeve across my mouth to get rid of the last crumb, when my dad asked me what day it was, I said 'Thursday'. He said 'no, it's half twelve, it's Friday'. Oh NO, I had sinned, I had eaten meat on Friday, I hoped that I didn't die before Saturday confessions.

My dad was a Prodi Dog. (Protestant) it was OK for him to eat meat. Catholicism was the one true faith, didn't they tell us that in school? But right then, I wished I was a protestant.

The party was still going strong when my dad decided it was late enough. We had a couple of miles to walk home, buses had stopped running and there was never any mention of a taxi. As we walked home in the moonlight, tired and happy, each of us holding my dad's hand, I felt like the richest girl in the world. We sang songs together from the pantomime. But the ribald songs from the party, we saved for the school playground.

FLITTING FROM THE SLUMS

November 1964

The address of the house we lived in, in Salford was 9 Muslinet Street, Salford 5.

These houses had been mass constructed 200 years before to house the Influx of people, fleeing poverty, hoping to find work in the mills springing up all over the north of England. Hence the street name "Muslinet" one of the types of cotton bringing wealth to Mill Owners of the 18th century.

These back-to-back terraced houses, by the 1900s, were classed as slums. They were damp, Clothes hanging in wardrobes, or put away in drawers would become mouldy. There was a coal fire in the front room, with an oven at one side and a shelf holding an iron kettle at the other. This was our only means of baking, heat or hot water.

In the kitchen was a deep pot sink, Where we washed, laundered clothes, prepared vegetables and bathed small children. There was a table and chairs and a cupboard. We also had a two ring gas hob, one cold water tap, an outside toilet and two bedrooms.

In one bedroom was a double bed, and a baby's cot, a dressing table and a chest of drawers. This is where my mam and dad and my youngest brother slept. In the other bedroom there were 2 single beds, one set of bunk beds and a wardrobe. There was barely any room between the beds. Here I slept with my sister and 3 brothers. On the tiny landing at the top of the stairs was kept a chamber pot in case you needed the toilet in the middle of the night, and you didn't fancy going out into the cold and dark back yard.

In the 1950s Salford began building houses in Little Hulton for people from these slums to "Flit" or relocate. The houses on the Mountskip Estate were built around about 1957. My auntie, uncle and cousin moved into a flat on Westway in 1963 and I often stayed with them at the weekend or school holidays.

In 1964 we were allocated a brand new 4 bedroom house on Westwood Avenue, it was like a dream come true. A semi-detached house with a garden. A living room, kitchen, wash house and a coal shed. There were three coal fires , One in the living room, one in the kitchen and one in the master bedroom. We were excited to see, not only a bathroom, but also a downstairs toilet. My brother Perry, aged 3 at the time, walked around telling anyone that would listen "two taps, two toilets"

On the day of the move, Salford Council provided huge lorries to take us to our new home. They allocated one lorry for two houses. Many people in those days had only one bed in each bedroom. Children and adults often "top and tailed" and winter coats used as blankets. My parents were different, when they learned of the move, they bought two new divan beds for my sister and me. And so there was a total of 7 beds loaded into the lorry. My mam had been stockpiling food and coal in case she struggled to pay the rent in the new house and my dad's bus fares to work. Up to that point he had lived close enough to walk home for his dinner each day. Therefore by the time all of our worldly goods, including coal was loaded into the back of the lorry there was barely room for us - yes that's right, Mother and 6 kids aged between 3 and 13 sat amongst the pots, pans, and prams. Tables chairs and clothes, toys and food etc etc. There was no room for the other family that was supposed to travel with us. Mam was crying because she was moving 9 miles away from the Salford she loved. She had waved my dad off to work that morning, telling him that they couldn't afford for him to have a day off.

The van driver and his mate were so impressed with this young mum (she would have been 34) with her 6 beautiful?? polite children, that they went above and beyond helping her to carry everything into our new house. They carried furniture, helped to put together beds and laid down carpets. The carpets emphasised how small the house we had moved from was, because what had been a fitted living room carpet, now had a big gap around the edge.

My mam was always proud to say that by the time she saw my dad striding across the fields from Manchester Road, tired after a hard day's graft and a long journey home, and probably not looking forward to having to build beds and move furniture. She could tell him that everything was done, the fire lit in the grate and his dinner was on the table. No wonder he loved her.

Each of the Estates of Little Hulton had been carefully planned. Each had a Catholic and a Protestant primary school, shops, laundrette, and doctors surgery. There were also three Secondary Modern schools within walking distance. Most people at that time didn't possess a car but for the ones that did, garages had been built.

But as ever in these situations, there had to be a problem. The Little Hultoners were wary of the Salford Overspill and the Salfordians were not in a rush to befriend the locals. Talking to a local priest one day he reported that Salfordians told him that when they had lived in Salford, they had never had any need to lock their doors, but now they had to, because they couldn't trust the locals. Funnily enough the people from Little Hulton reported that they had never had to lock their doors until these Salford People moved here.

In the early 1980s My parents were able to buy their house, and despite the fact that they have both since passed away, it still remains in the family.

Childhood Maladies

So many childhood ailments of which to bemoan
I reflected with my Dad when I was fully grown
'You had everything but the mange' he said
All too often in childhood I was confined to bed
Rest being considered best all round therapy
In all instances for a full and final recovery
Apart from chicken pox, measles and mumps
Leaving my four brothers down in the dumps
They did not ail; which baffled Mum and Dad
As whilst I would tuck into what they also had
Such as soups and stews and porridge with salt
The boys were finicky so substituted with malt
They pulled such faces as the extract went down
Though orange juice took away any lingering frown
Issued by Ministry of Health along with cod liver oil
Their post-World War Two intention was to foil
Procreation of a sickly malnourished next generation
Did not reckon with me when strengthening a nation
Born three weeks overdue with septic fingers and eyes
Consequently suffered from eczema all through my life
Oft at Manchester & Salford Hospital for Skin Diseases
And Gartside Street Outpatients to investigate wheezes
So many times suffered earache and tonsillitis, it is said
One feverish night, the devil was sat at the end of my bed
A guarded open fire in Hospital Ward when tonsils removed
Eased by a bowl of ice cream but this operation later reproved
As strep infection with no throat protection led to rheumatic fever
Confined for many months with a cage over my legs as a reliever
Upon recovery, my childhood years were over and soon
Into Beatlemania, Civil Rights, Quant fashion and jobs boom

ROSEMARY SWIFT

Teenage years

PAUL HALLOWS

I once worked at Princes Park Garden Centre in Irlam. On V.E day we built an air raid shelter and turned it into a mini museum. We placed various things in there like a gas mask, a soldier's helmet and some more things. People were allowed to go in and have a look around.

We also had to dress up as soldiers. I think it was the same day I met the bloke who wrote *The Blackpool Belle,* an old folk song. His name was Howard Broadbent.

Sometime later when I went to Bolton Market Radio I met his sister Dorothy who ran the radio station. I learnt a lot of skills from the radio station which have been useful now at Salford City Radio 94.4fm.

Air Crash 1957

COLIN BALMER

I have never claimed a good memory. One of the most momentous events at primary school needed extensive research to fill in some of the gaps and further imaginative rumination to resolve the queries that arose.

On March 14, 1957, within a week of my eleventh birthday, I was in class in my final year at Shadow Moss C of E Primary School on Ringway Road, Moss Nook. This was the fateful day when a BEA Viscount airliner crashed into houses on Shadow Moss Road, Wythenshawe, killing twenty two people. My school was only a few hundred yards from the disaster, but I cannot remember hearing or seeing anything of the accident with the loss of all fifteen passengers, five crew and a mother and child living in one of the houses. I can remember being escorted home along with classmates by a more senior monitor. The school was evacuated and used as a hospital and mortuary for the crash victims. The date confirms that I was eleven years old, I had sat and passed my 11+ for grammar school, so I must have been one of the more senior pupils at the school. Why did I, then, need an escort to prevent my curiosity drawing me to the crash? Possibly headmistress Mrs Ashworth felt a Cheshire girl would make a more responsible chaperone for the children than a boy from the council estate. I also held a responsible position as ink monitor.

I also remember there was a period when I attended St Anthony's Primary School to give me a better Roman Catholic foundation before moving on to Xaverian College Grammar School. So why was I still at the C of E primary school in March? This short spell must have been after the crash. I cannot recall going back to Shadow Moss School, other than an embarrassing visit to give the headmistress a bunch of flowers. The day that the BEA Viscount came down might possibly have been my last before transition to St Anthony's.

My strongest memory of St Anthony's was getting the strap for running on the stairs. No such corporal chastisement had been used at my former school. However, there were no stairs in the old three-classroom building anyway.

It was some time after being taken home that I ventured on to the crash site and picked up a morbid souvenir in a small piece of aluminium. I doubt that the chance would be given now in days of intensive forensic investigation. It did not, at the time, register with me that our school had been in the flight path of flight 411 from Amsterdam and the day could have been the last for everyone in school. Nobody knows what happened in the cockpit but witness reports tell that the aircraft made a sudden right turn around a mile from the runway after clearing low clouds with landing gear lowered. In a steep downward angle, the wing tip touched the ground; the plane broke up, burst into flames and crashed into the row of houses. Mechanical failure was suspected as the cause of the accident and BEA grounded some 25 of its fleet after the incident.

I went on to grow up in Woodhouse Park and witnessed the growth of the airport and Wythenshawe. I moved away when I married in 1971. Since then family and friends in Wythenshawe have all died or moved out, so I have no need to visit the area these days. The houses have been rebuilt, leaving no sign of the tragedy. My old school has been demolished as the airport expanded and you would never know of the dreadful disaster as your tram takes you along Shadow Moss Road towards Manchester International Airport.

Childhood Rainy Days

Although it sounds trite, old hat or simply absurd
Childhood memories can often be stirred by a word
For the sake of this exercise, the example is RAIN
Such as a race of drops sliding down a windowpane
Or watching a heavy shower through an open door
Whilst sat on stairs pretending to drive a bus or train
As the abating storm trickled its way down a drain
Heavy sleet had bounced giant hailstones around
Rattling empty milk bottles left out on the ground
Lightning often struck fear and thunder would roar
At storm's end appeared a rainbow of many a hue
That then wept its colours into a sky of plain blue
In the garden, frogs leapt and earthworms wriggled
Flowers bore heavy dew whilst butterflies jiggled
The sun beamed down, master of the sky once more
'Mam, can I play out again now' was often the cry
From the kitchen could be heard, with a heavy sigh
'Put on your wellie-bobs and a coat with a hood
You coming down with a fever will do me no good
Oh, after jumping in puddles keep off my clean floor!'

ROSEMARY SWIFT

Growing Up in Little Hulton

CHRIS MUTTON

Before 1949 Little Hulton was a village of around 8,000 people and then Worsley Urban District Council agreed to the building of council estates for people living in post-war slum clearance areas. By the end of 1956 over a thousand families had moved into the area. By 1962, 3,060 houses had been built. I can still remember the division between the two disparate communities. I can't see that the use of the term 'overspill' helped, nor did the reputation of people from Salford as 'rough' or the belief that the Little Hulton local folk were yokels. I remember an atmosphere very much of 'us and them' - on both sides.

I remember being taken to look at the foundations of some of the new houses that were being built on Captain Fold, one summer Saturday evening, on one of our regular family walks. This is just one of certain events, people, buildings and places that feature in my memories of being a child in Little Hulton during this time.

When I was a child, Little Hulton was an insular place to grow up. I lived on Manchester Road East. We seldom crossed over Cleggs Lane to Manchester Road West, even though there were shops there. Of these, Timm's Chemist was one place visited on a Sunday when there weren't any doctors surgeries open. People used to queue to get in, so good was his reputation of being as good as, if not better than, the regular GPs. Further along was Peel Park which was sometimes visited with our parents on a Saturday night. We would go from there to The Kenyon Arms Pub where we would sit outside whilst Dad had a pint, Mum a shandy and my brother and I a lemonade with a bag of Smith's crisps - containing a blue twisted bag of salt to be added to the plain crisps. Sometimes this little bag was omitted but sometimes it just couldn't be found - until scooped, with a handful of crisps into an unsuspecting mouth. If this happened to us we gained little sympathy and were told it served us right for putting more than one crisp in our mouths at a time. I'm not sure if we were supposed to eat them one at a time for good manners, thrift or to keep us quiet for longer. My Dad was a hod-carrier for Seddons, for most of his working life, and had worked on the rebuilding of this pub, my Mum told us that he had built it - and I literally thought he had done it single-handedly for years. (He also built The Lucozade Factory by himself)

There were other shops on this row but the only one I can remember going in is the shoe shop that sold Clarks shoes. Even though money was tight we always got our shoes from there because our feet were measured before a purchase was made. I remember peering through the window of Taziker's Newsagents, which also sold toys - maybe that's why we didn't go in there. We did go to the churchyard at St Paul's Peel to visit the grave of my paternal grandparents. This always felt very daring because, as Catholics, we weren't supposed to visit other denominations' churches. My Dad wasn't Catholic and used to get really cross when I worried over this as a child. As an adult I completely understand why.

Back on our side of the lane we had all the little shops we needed. Bessie Tyldesley's bread and cake shop - all made by her, was on the corner of the next row and the row after that had corner shops at either end. One was called Harrisons and one Halinsons. There is a tale to be told for both of these shops concerning my childhood. Outside Halinsons was where my mother left me in my pram when I was newborn. She'd been there in the morning and gone home. A few hours later she thought she should be 'doing something' and then realised that the 'something' was feeding me! She dashed back there to find me still safely sleeping - the owners had kept their eye on me and told her they had wondered how long it would take her to realise she'd left me. Harrison's event was when I was older. We had a kitten, which I decided to dress in my doll's matinee coat and take for a walk in my doll's pram. I went into Harrisons, with the cat in the pram, which the cat then jumped out of and into their shop window - demolishing the displays. I think I was actually banned from there as a result by them or my Mum, I'm not sure. For larger items and bigger food shops was The Co-operative, at the corner of Cleggs Lane. I remember being sent there on errands chanting my Mum's divi number so I wouldn't forget, - I can remember it to this day! The Co-op was a building of some merit, architecturally. It consisted of different departments on the ground floor and a large assembly room above - this was where my mother used to go ballroom dancing and where I would, years later, in the 1970's, also go to dance, when it became Uncle Tom's Cabin.

I lived in a terraced house on the A6, at one end was a newsagents, owned by Mr and Mrs Hunt for many years, I remember her as a lovely smiling lady and not going into the shop when her grumpy husband was serving. It was from there that our Easter Eggs, fireworks and Christmas sweets and annuals were bought. On the end of the row before that was Kay's Off Licence which sold spirits, beer and draught sherry - Dad used to take a jug for this when mum was making her egg whip - a concoction of raw eggs, Nestles Condensed Milk and sherry - supposedly a tonic. At Christmas we had QC sweet sherry and a bottle of their port. On Friday nights, we had a bottle of Lemonade or Dandelion and Burdock with a bag of crisps, provided we'd been good through the week. At the back of our row of terraces were huge corrugated hangers which housed the large delivery wagons belonging to Kays'. As children we always had to leave the backs at 4pm and go into our gardens because that's when the lorries left. I can still vividly remember one occasion, but not how old I was, when myself and my two playmates - both also called Christine, held a tea party - under one of these lorries which had left the depot but stopped whilst the driver went back in. He was just entering the cabin to drive off when we were spotted and dragged out - and into our respective homes, being shaken and admonished as we went. In later years the hangers were demolished and Bulmers Cider's wholesale warehouse was built. As the building work took place, houses were overrun with field mice - we didn't suffer because we had a cat, in fact the neighbours used to come and borrow her. I vaguely remember a smug smile on my Mum's face when she explained why the cat was suddenly so popular.

Opposite our row of houses, where the Madams' Wood Estate now is, were Bluebell Woods and fields that used to stretch to Mosley Common. As children we frequently walked to a place called City, which consisted of a row of houses and a phone box. Another freedom we enjoyed was being able to spend all day roaming on our bicycles. I would frequently turn up at my favourite Auntie Ann and Uncle Mac's house in Walkden, prop my bike against their house wall and spend the rest of the day with them. They had moved from a prefab house on Pemberton Street Little Hulton to a new council house on Sportside Avenue and I thought they were very modern and 'posh'. I loved them both and was always made to feel welcome. Sadly, Uncle Mac, my dad's brother, died in his early thirties due to kidney disease and the lack of dialysis machines.

Walkden was considered considerably better than Little Hulton. I first remember going to The Criterion Cinema with my Mum, who worked there for a short time, as an usherette, to see Annie Get Your Gun and Tammy, both musicals and starring Doris Day. I sat on the back row on the edge of the upturned seat -I remember being there and small sections of the films but have no idea why I would be there at night time with her. I can also remember going, and queuing, with her (dressed in our 'best' clothes) to the opening of Kenton's Supermarket - a first of its kind in the area. After this, we must have shopped there more often because I remember looking through the windows of The Journal Office, at the bottom of Bolton Road, to see if I could spot 'Uncle George' who judged the children's weekly colouring competition, crayoning up to a certain age (was it seven?) and painting after that. I only won once. Across the road from this was a row of terraced shops under a Victorian Veranda: The only ones I remember are Middleton's Grocers, (we didn't go in there, my mum said it was dirty) which later became the Journal Office when shops on the other side were demolished and Mr Lever's Jewellers shop.

For me, as a child, other trips to Walkden were to the Palace Picture House on a Saturday morning. I received a shilling spending money, (5p). This was for bus fare - penny ha'penny each way, threepence for sweets - usually two ounces of pineapple chunks or pear drops and sixpence to get in the cinema. But, first, we queued to be let in a few at a time, kept in order by the long suffering usherettes -and their arm, as it shot out to let us know when to stop, often knocking the breath out of the one who got 'the arm'. Once through the main doors, the queue made an orderly rush into the downstairs part of the theatre, with its plush seats and impressive ornate facades, all of which we ignored. Anticipation and excitement grew as we waited impatiently for the films to begin. We shouted, cheered and laughed as we watched the programme made up of films, cartoons and always a serial, which ended on a cliff hanger to ensure we returned the following week. We always did - the cinema was full every week in those pre television days. We watched Daffy Duck, Bugs Bunny and my favourite, Porky Pig. I'm sure we saw a black and white version of Batman and Robin and some weeks, William Tell. There was also The Three Stooges and Our Gang, which starred the young Mickey Rooney.

As I got older the cinema was replaced by the more sedate pursuit of ballroom dancing lessons, at Turner's Dancing Academy - a large garage type building built at the side of their house. This was just outside of the town centre, on the way to Swinton - foreign land! Also on the way to Swinton, in Wardley was my Godparent's farm where I stayed for a week. I fed the chickens and was frightened of the cows. I hated using the outside chemical toilet but loved going to bed because Auntie Margaret left me a small present under my pillow every night - what a clever idea! I remember one was a child's thumb size book that had concertinaed pages and another a viewer which I clicked to move pictures round. Both contained holy pictures. As my ambition, at the time, was to be a nun, I was delighted with them.

In those days all our neighbours were borrowed aunties and uncles, I never knew my Grandparents - they all died within eighteen months of one another, my Paternal Grandad just months before I was born, So the elderly lady in the end house was my borrowed Grandma and I called her Nanna Brookes. She had a pug dog which permanently slavered and Grandad Brookes always smoked a pipe so their house smelled of pipe smoke and tobacco. She had a chenille table cloth and a matching door curtain and a Grandchild called Elspeth who I envied - not only for her exotic name but because she was Nanna Brooke's real Granddaughter. My other 'Nanna' was Mrs Collier, who also lived on Manchester Road East, a five - ten minute walk from our house. We used to go to visit her on our way home from school, she made me a Davy Crockett Hat from her old fur coat. I wore it all the time - even to bed. It was at this time that I started to have nightmares, usually about Mohicans and knives. My Mum took me to the Doctor's, who recommended that my parents take away all my books as I had an overactive imagination- my Dad took away my beloved hat but left the books.

People's doors were left open in those days, if it rained a neighbour took your washing in for you, if your line snapped everyone rushed to help. Help was also there whenever someone was ill - especially if it was the mother. For all that, we weren't encouraged to go into other people's houses, in fact rather the opposite. The house I went to most was my friend Christine's, but not as often as she came to mine, much to my mum's annoyance. There we read her flower fairy book - I never got to have one of those because it would look like 'copying' but I loved them (my daughter had the full set!) and,of course, we played with our paper dolls dressing up sets. I was envious of two things: They had Fray Bentos tinned Steak and Kidney Pie - my Mother was apoplectic when I suggested we have one because we had home made everything. The second was their wall ornament - a 'plate' made from Capstan Full Strength cigarette packets, folded in such a way that it was a circle of the captain's heads. I was always welcome next door to Auntie Annie and Uncle Tom's. Possibly because she had three sons, Martin, Michael and Kevin, and, according to my Mum, had always wanted a girl. My source of envy from this property was their leaded windows AND three ducks that flew in a diagonal line up the wall. I never understood my Mum's refusal to get us some - I thought they were wonderful. They were also the first people to get a television set. It was a 12" black and white one with one channel, The BBC. In 1960 their front room was packed as we all crowded in to watch Princess Margaret get married. We didn't get a set until 1966 when we rented one from Rediffusion - just in time for my brother to watch the World Cup. We weren't supposed to go to Aunty Margery and Uncle Stan's who lived in the house next to the newsagents - because she was too lazy to get a milk jug but rather put a milk bottle on the table. We weren't invited to go into Aunty Alice and Uncle Stan's (they were

Georgie Fame's Auntie and Uncle but I only knew that when he turned up on their daughter's wedding day) possibly because they didn't have children the same age as us.

People didn't have house phones in those days. Mobiles hadn't been thought of - even in my much loved science fiction films, where computers filled rooms and tried to rule the world. But my parents always knew where I had been, who with and exactly what I had been doing. In a different world to today, we had the freedom to explore and run free within a community which looked after its own, related or not. Freedoms that our children, sadly, never knew.

Billy-O and Cheekee

John Newton

John Newton lived in Salford before emigrating to Perth Western Australia in 1964 as a young boy of ten.. Today he resides in Perth with his wife Allison and two children Clifton and Jennifer. This is an abridged extract from his collection 'Summer of 1963 – Field of Dreams'

John Lawton, as I was known to the local people of Swinton, was a tearaway. If asked most would say it all started when he was 11 years old and, looking back, I would have to agree with them.

It was a glorious July day in 1963 as my little legs propelled me towards the moss fields, watching the butterflies flit from grass to hedge as I whizzed by jumping over the puddles left from the night's rain. I waited for what seemed to be ages before Star the horse could be coaxed to come over to the rails for the moist clump of grass I had tugged out of the earth, a pat on his snout and off I went.

Now passing the ducks and pigs kept by farmer Dyson. Oh! Life's great as I pick up speed heading towards the Red Bridge. Golden wheat fields glimmering in the morning sun as the Red Bridge comes into sight, but trains no longer run here - unless you have the imagination of a ten year old, then anything is possible including German soldiers making their way through the wheat fields to conquer my beloved town or a chance meeting with Tom Sawyer on the banks of the Mississippi River which, of course, was really the River Irwell. The bridge is different today as many people are crossing it, all going in the one direction. When I arrive at the bridge I quickly climb the embankment and almost trip over a group of five children moving along with the throng, expectation and determination written all over their faces.

'Hey, what's going on?'

125

But no one answers me, then at the last minute a girl of my age turns around and blurts out,

'The Lucozade factory has burnt down and we are all bound to go and get some drinks and chockies. Best you come or I'm telling you you'll miss out.'

'What's your name?'

'It's Hannah.'

'How come you wear jeans?'

'Cos I'm a tomboy. That's why silly! If you split your drinks and chockies with me, I'll let you call me by my nickname. Only very special friends can call me it though, so will you split your drinks and chockies with me?'

'Yes I will Hannah'

'Good, then you can call me Cheekee.'

'OK Cheekee it is then.'

'What's your name then?'

'It's John.'

'And your nickname?'

'Well I don't really have one.'

'Well I'll just have to make one up for you. Yikes, c'mon they are getting in front of us; we will have to go like Billy O to catch up. Hmmm I may have a nickname for you, John.'

We had travelled three and half miles to arrive at the slag heaps between Sandow Pit and Walkden. We could see the trucks tipping the unspoilt produce over one of the large hills. Oh what a sight! Men women and children clambering up the hill to eagerly gather up the drinks and chocolates before putting them into bags and some into old prams that they had brought along to take the booty home.

Prompted by Hannah I scrambled up the hill for our share of the spoils. In no time at all we had filled a large carrier bag to the top with everything from Smarties to Lucozade.

126

Our hands each gripped one of the handles of the bag as we headed back home. The road seemed so much longer going back and our young legs began to tire.

'Let's sit for a while,' said Cheekee.

We sat down on the grassed embankment overlooking the fields towards Kearsley.

'I still think we have a ways to go before we reach home Hannah.'

'Yep we do,' she said as we turned our heads sidewards to look at what seemed an endless track that disappeared into the distance.

'Here.' she said, passing me a bottle of Lucozade from the bag.

A little suspicious of getting anything for free, we watched each other as we drank down the drink.

'It tastes lovely, John.'

'Yes it does and look how much we got. My mam will be so pleased.'

Now munching on Smarties, the tomboy asks, 'How much you done then?'

'What do you mean?'

'Well Billy…'

'Hey me name's not Billy'

'Yep, it is. That's your nickname Billy the Kid.'

'Well, I don't like the kid bit.'

I could see her thinking and her eyes lit up as she said, 'It's Billy O. That's what it will be from now on Billy O. So what I'm asking you Billy O is have you ever been on the Moss after dark?'

'Nope, I ain't.'

'Well then, have you ever been in the cemetery on your own?'

'Nope, I ain't.'

Then she asked me something that I **had** done.

'Well have you ever been on the swing over the valley at Clifton woods?'

'Yep, yep. I done that.'

'OK, Billy O which one?'

'The one near the church.'

She looked at me for a second, flicked back her long auburn hair and at the same time started to laugh. 'What's funny?' I said, feeling awkward and at the same time thinking 'I don't know if I like this girl.'

'Well John, that swing's for little kids. We use the big one in the second valley and I'll take you there one day but you mustn't say owt cos mi brothers say to keep it a secret. Have you ever been to Pear Tree Farm?'

'No, I ain't, Cheekee.'

'Well I'll take you there as well. Now c'mon we best get going home or mi Mam and Dad won't let me out if I get home late.'

The sun was setting and our little legs aching as we finally walked off the Moss. We stopped at the cemetery wall to split up the drinks and chocolates.

'Now don't forget Billy-O. Redbridge next Satdy and remember not a word to anyone and don't forget to bring a big jumper,'

'What for Hannah?'

'You will have to wait and see Billy-O. See ya. Tarraaaaa.'

I went to bed that night thinking, 'I've made a good friend. I like her and she was different from the other girls I know and it didn't matter that she was a bit bossy.'

I couldn't wait for next Saturday, but in the meantime I had to persuade Mam to get me a pair of jeans like Hannah's from the markets - the ones with two back pockets cos that's the style now.

'Goodnight John. Did you have a good day?'

'Yeah I did, Mam.'

'That's my boy and not an ounce of trouble.'

128

The Family Clock

ROSEMARY SWIFT

The day my Dad was born in Stockport, his Dad, having called into a second-hand shop, brought home as a gift for the baby a grandmother wall clock.

My Dad always maintained he could remember his birth: '*The sun was streaming down the lobby which I could see from the open parlour door.*' He was 14 lbs born (so was my future husband) and quite poorly for a while (as was my husband – it cannot be natural to be born that weight).

Upon marriage, my Dad hung his clock in the living room of the rented terraced house in inner-city Manchester but when, as an eventual family of seven, we moved to the suburbs my Mum tucked the clock under the stairs as she set to decorating the house, culminating with her running up fibreglass curtains. She disposed of the old-fashioned gate-legged dining room table and replaced it with a Formica-topped kitchen table. My Dad's clock was not going to fit in with the height of 1960s fashion.

After my Mum died, my Dad downsized and as I was married, living in an Edwardian house at Irlams o'th' Height, my Dad gave me the clock and it looked just the thing in the hallway for many a year. Upon my husband and I downsizing to a bungalow, it is now prominent in my lounge alongside sepia family photographs. Through the years, I have on occasions offered it to my four brothers but none were bothered. Two are now dead, the eldest lives in a tiny Didsbury cottage and my third brother lives in Hayfield; both have homes where the clock would suit.

When I retired from work, I started as a hobby researching family trees (although sadly all senior members of my family were then deceased). To my amazement, I found that members of my Dad's paternal family over a few generations had been clockmakers. I purchased a book entitled 'Clockmakers of

129

Cheshire' where there are examples of Kellett clocks portraying colourful sun dials set in impressive casings.

My paternal Grandfather, from an early age, was not raised by his father, Samuel Kellett, but rather by Charles Hobson so when upon marriage he was told he could not marry in the name of Hobson he baulked and was thus allowed to register as John Kellett-Hobson. This double-barrelled name was borne by his three sons and my older cousins. It was dropped for my four brothers and I as my Dad, being very much the socialist, declared it was too fanciful so we were registered with the surname of Hobson only whereas the bloodline is Kellett.

My Dad's maternal grandparents, paternal grandfather and foster grandfather all died before his birth but he had fond memories of his Dad's Mum. A feisty Armagh-born lady, she would walk every Saturday carrying a basket of fruit from Heaton Norris to Ancoats to visit her son and his family. My Mum would tut regarding the act of favouritism when my Dad laughingly related how his Grandma Eliza would polish the reddest rosiest apple on her pinny for my Dad saying *that's for the flower of the flock*.

My Dad's Dad was an overseer at Murray's Mill in Ancoats and in earlier years had swapped between there and its sister mill in Stockport; so much so, he had met and married my Sale-Moor born Grandma (of Mayo stock) when both were working in Manchester and had a Manchester-born eldest son. They then returned to Stockport where my Dad was born. Then back to Manchester for good where his third son was born.

The origin of my surname was not a shock when I was researching my family tree, I had grown up with the knowledge but now I was faced with the possibility perhaps my clock had some value.

So when Antiques Roadshow came to Salford Quays in August 2018, my husband and I struggled down with this unwieldy large wall clock with its pendulum clanging, only to be dismissed with it having a moderate value, being mass-produced in Bavaria and sold widespread in late Victorian England. As of now it probably has an age of some 140 years so it can be classed as an antique but its monetary value cannot be matched as to how much I treasure it in memory of my lovely Dad and his Cheshire roots.

My First Job

CHRIS VICKERS

Listening to the news on the radio I heard that TSB were laying off a number of staff. The mention of TSB sent me on a reverie, as I began my working life in the late 1960s, as a callow 16 year old, employed at my local branch, Irlams O'th' Height. This came about because I left school with three O' levels and absolutely no idea of what I wanted to do or clear direction from elsewhere, although my English teacher, Jock Weir, urged my parents to let me stay on at school.

Bizarrely, my Grandad who had moved in to live with us had a word with the manager of the neighbourhood TSB, Dean Clayton, about employing me and so I met him for a 'chat come interview' and ended up being offered a job. Any job in banking in those days was considered safe, solid: 'a job for life'.

So it was I drifted into 'penny banking' administering and safeguarding the savings of the local community: butchers, bakers and world famous referees! More of that later.

Following a short period at the Height branch I transferred to Pendlebury, a bus ride from home. The manager was old school, meticulous in manner and fastidious in dress. He was also a dead ringer for Captain Mainwaring from Dad's Army. The branch was delightful in many ways not least by a sense of camaraderie fostered by the manager. Staff were addressed by him, and by extension each other as MR Christopher, MISS Sue, MR Brian, MR Laurence and so on. Togetherness seemed to ensue, helped possibly by the custom of buying cream cakes for all on birthdays.

In those days Securicor didn't deliver to branches and consequently every Monday morning I reported to Head Office on Booth Street, Manchester where I would meet the deputy manager, Mr Brian. Inside the grand building an assembly of 2ICs gathered to collect the cash required for their branches for the week ahead.

Incredibly we met at 0900 every Monday and cash was bundled into old pages of the Financial Times, and tied with string. I was the poster boy of striplings and Mr Brian had a 'gammy' leg. To top it off we drove with the money from central Manchester to Pendlebury in his Messerschmidt three wheel bubble car!

In short order I became a counter clerk taking in deposits and paying out cash as required. At least my arithmetic improved as at the close of business one had to add up handwritten ledgers of some forty or so figures…and balance. On busy afternoons the bank would be packed and clerks had to shout out customer names and effect the transaction. I recall one occasion shouting: 'Mrs Sidebottom'. Once the branch had closed and I was balancing my books the manager sidled over and rebuked me: 'Now, Mr Christopher the pronunciation is Mrs Side- Botham'. One of my favourite customers was a thoroughly pleasant, easy going guy who always had time for a word. It transpired that he was one of the very best referees England has ever produced, Neil Midgely.

One Monday morning I rocked up to the branch and found it thronged with police and bemused colleagues. Excitingly there'd been an attempted break-in the night before. The robbery had been bungled but the police took staff details and fingerprinted us all anyway.

I stayed at the bank for six years and remain friends to this day with Mr Laurence who forged a great banking career moving to work in the Isle of Man. Ultimately, despite studying bank exams, it wasn't for me and I found salvation in the oil industry.

Holiday Snapshots

ROSEMARY SWIFT

As a child, my playmates and I emulated the antics of the Famous Five and Secret Seven in inner-city Manchester which Enid Blyton would have had no knowledge of. Nor indeed did we have access to the scenery outlined by her. And when later I was immersed in the book 'Swallows & Amazons' it did not mean I hankered to go to the Lake District - I was grateful for whatever holiday trip came along.

My earliest memory of such is excitedly running under the arches near London Road Station (now Manchester Piccadilly BR) to reach the platform to board a steam train hissing and puffing. There is more than one photograph of myself and brothers at different ages (wearing circular name badges) to realise we must have gone to Middleton Towers in Morecambe on at least two occasions. Another haunt favoured by Mum and Dad for an annual weekly break was Cleveleys.

I also remember running over the Red Rec (recreation ground) near my Beswick home to reach a row of Claribel Coaches off Ashton Old Road. This mode of transport for day trips would have been used by the family before I can remember as my Dad told of pushing myself and my cousin Barry in the same pram (again I have a photograph) over the sands at Blackpool or Southport. My Dad cherished my Mum and took on any physical strain as she had valvular heart disease as did her younger sister Marian but her husband was probably off playing cricket for his work's team. As I got older, I can remember the challenge of becoming the first to spot Blackpool Tower – which became heated, especially with my brother Mike who was a poor loser.

My brothers and I were never denied school trips, which is probably why I cannot remember going away as a family on week-long holidays as we grew older, the money being needed for whichever child came home to tell of a school excursion. When aged about 10, my eldest brother Greg went to Lowestoft for a week. Upon his return, everyone stifled laughter when he produced a jar of Brylcreem and a tin of toothpaste powder as gifts for Dad and maternal Grandad who lived next door – they were both bald and wore dentures!

My brothers Mike and Steve seemed content with regular scouts' camps. My youngest brother Des once went to London and I was so proud of a photo of him with his teachers and schoolmates taken outside the Houses of Parliament. He also went on an educational-boat for a week that sailed around the Baltic Sea, embarking at various ports.

With primary-school, I went to Knokke in Belgium, at age 11, where an exquisite doll was handed in for me at the Hotel by a family my Dad had befriended during World War Two. I also went on a secondary-school holiday to Middelburg in Belgium at age 15 and remember dodging hundreds of jellyfish on the beach. On the sailing back, it was announced that Marilyn Monroe had died.

Apart from the above mentioned weekly breaks there was many a day trip which I enjoyed just as much. With bottles of sherbet-flavoured water and jam butties, myself, brothers and neighbourhood pals would set off for nearby Philip's Park which we also went to with parents on Tulip Sunday – an annual, much anticipated, event. Opened 22 August 1846, this park was a favourite of my Mum and Dad growing up and who had married locally on 22 August 1942.

135

We went on the bus to my cousin Barry's in Moston and roamed nearby Boggart Hole Clough. Or we would board a trolley bus on Ashton New Road to visit older cousins in Droylsden. Once, I came back to my Uncle's home on the shoulders of my cousin Celia having lost my shoes in deep mud on the Moss which backed their rear garden. It seemed a long way to go on the 103 bus to my cousins' in Woodhouse Park, Wythenshawe who all knew not to talk whilst aeroplanes roared over their rooftop from the then Ringway Airport. They had a massive green at the front of their home on which we played for hours.

A regular annual outing was to Poynton Fair and then on for tea nearby at my Dad's cousin Theresa's; there was always a doily-covered dish emitting a strong vinegary smell of home-made pickled onions and cucumber. A rarer treat was to nearby Belle Vue as it was an expensive day out for a family of seven, especially when we mithered for a ride on an elephant.

When we moved to the suburbs, our house overlooked Fog Lane Park which contained tennis courts, football pitches and an animal corner. When my Dad came home after a night shift at GPO Parcel Post, he did not like hearing the peacocks as the sound always reminded him of a child crying. Viewed from our front window, sometimes there was a larger crowd than usual around the football pitches. This was when Corinthian Ladies played – they had to battle against prejudice in their early years but their ultimate success was measured by many trophies in the window of the local Fish & Chips shop.

During school breaks (to allow my Dad much needed sleep) my Mum would take my brothers and me to such as Platt Fields (and its Costume Gallery) or Wythenshawe Hall or Vernon Park (also known as Pinch-Belly Park, built by hungry, out-of-work mill workers in 1850s). Near Bredbury (where my Dad's fraternal folk originated from) its high walls are similar to those of Langworthy Road Chimney Pot Park.

On a nice summer's evening, as a family, we occasionally toddled along to Northenden as far as the River Mersey. On one such outing my Mum turned round on Parrs Wood Road to see me tottering on stiletto heels - I was ordered home to change to suitable footwear.

My friend Angela and I would board an electric-line train at Burnage Station to spend a few hours in and around Styal Woods. Once, we played hooky from Secretarial College (rare, as we were keen students) to visit Chester Zoo on a scorching hot summer day. Soon after that when we started work, we booked a caravan in Prestatyn only for it to pour with rain all week – we knew one another so well that we did not need to talk and spent all the time reading, stretched out on divan seats.

I often stayed at my Aunt Sheila's off Middleton Road and would take her four children to nearby Heaton Park. A school friend's father was employed there and they lived in a dilapidated tied cottage, within the park's grounds, lit only by oil lamps until they were housed circa 1960 off Victoria Avenue. Sounds exciting but it could be quite spooky at nightfall.

In May 1970, whilst my husband Archie was in Aberystwyth with Salford Lads Club at their annual Whit camp, I returned to what had been Middleton Towers in Morecambe, which had become a Pontins Holiday Camp, with my Mum, Dad and maternal grandparents. My Mum's sister Sheila and her daughter, my cousin, Helen should have joined us but Sheila was whipped into hospital for a mastectomy which thankfully proved successful. This was to be my last 'childhood' holiday as at the following Whit Week of 1971, when I had just celebrated my 24th birthday (and not yet had children of my own) my lovely Mum died the day after heart surgery... and I grew up!

A Four Suit Education

COLIN BALMER

I grew up in the fifties in a new three-bedroom council house in Woodhouse Park, Wythenshawe. At the time, Wythenshawe in South Manchester was the world's largest council developement. Like most of the young families in the area we enjoyed life without much in the way of luxury. Toys were a mixture of precious shop bought treasures and imaginative constructions from something else. Pram wheels, for example, were the prized basis of many a street machine. Would today's generation still use the expression upcycling to describe the metamorphosis of bit of tree into a Western cowboy's Colt '45?

In our house, my brother, sister and I were introduced, at a tender age, to classic children's games like Snakes and Ladders, Ludo and Draughts and learned the joys of competition and the need for rules. Our academic learning was given an important boost by playing pub games. I guess my Dad must have been the dartboard custodian of the Airport Hotel as I can remember the log end soaking in a bucket in our wash house. I became adept with the wood and feather arrows long before I ventured into the local vaults as a drinking and darting teenager. Dominoes was a regular family evening's pleasure before TV was even considered a necessary domestic appliance. The mental arithmetic skills developed by these games put us in good stead at school, but the competitive element set us up for life in the world. Playing against grow-ups, who were neither condescending nor patronising, taught us how to handle success with magnanimity or to lose gracefully, whilst understanding the essences of co-operation.

Pub games cannot be mentioned without looking at the delights and imagination associated with handling a pack of 52 playing cards. Snap, Strip-Jack-Naked, Patience and Rummy taught co-ordination, concentration, relationships and patterns. The family game of Knock Out Whist enhanced such skills, while seducing

 the players with its increased complexity.

We were relatively young when left on a Friday night with a pack of cards or dominoes and a bottle of Woodpecker while our parents had their night out in the pub, Labour Club or Legion. As we matured, we learned grown-up card games from Mam and Dad. 'Fifteens' and 'Nines and Fives' were our household names for Crib and Nine-Card Don respectively. I know that this home education stood me well when I eventually accompanied Dad in 'The Airport' and was not disgraced on my first venture to the card table.

The best of pub card games exists in two forms Solo Whist and Napoleon. 'Solo', which uses all 52 cards and each player tries to beat the other three, combines knowledge, memory, concentration, some bravado and, naturally, a measure of luck. Solo is what I trust those friends who have gone before me will have taught Elvis when I take up my corner at the table in Paradise. The shorter more aggressive variation 'Nap' never held me in its thrall – being significantly luck based and generally more anti-social, because it is a gambling game. I think it was a blessing that serious gambling on card games was illegal in my formative years so competitive cards was more social. Stakes measured in coppers were the norm, although pub landlords would turn the same blind eye that never saw the bookies runner. Consequently, games like Poker and Brag were played behind closed curtains and latterly in Casinos after the *The Betting and Gaming Act act of 1960.*

Evacuation, North vs South

ALAN RICK

It was during the last year of the war in 1944 that it finally seemed to dawn on the government that hostility had commenced and hastily had us London children packed off to the provinces to escape the V2 rockets – Hitler's last gasp attempt to grab victory. My brother and I had no idea what evacuation entailed beyond our teacher's vague and disdainful explanation that we would be banished to 'The North'. This, we gathered, was some sort of limbo land you were sent to if you were seen as no longer fit for civilised society. But at least it would be better than the bombs. We were prepared for the first stage of the journey to the railway station, for transportation to we had no idea where, by the teacher, Mr Redman, who was not allowed to tell us the destination. This acquired an even more sinister aspect in our minds when we learnt that he would not be staying there, but would be returning to London once he had delivered us to the families who had agreed to take in evacuees.

Why were our parents to remain in London? We were convinced that we must have committed some grave misbehaviour to be sent parentless to what may as well have been a foreign country. Any place, in our minds, north of Middlesex was threatening territory.

Suitably dressed for travel in coats, trousers and shirts mainly handed down from older siblings and with boxed gas masks secured to our sides, we were marched to the railway station for our voyage into the unknown, a bedraggled picture of bewilderment and distrust. The government manufacturer of gas masks had ordered special, smaller versions to be made for primary school children. Mine had a Mickey Mouse on the outside, apparently intended to mark the child size gas mask. The cautionary gas mask drill exercise was supervised by the Headmaster who would strike fear into us by describing, with staring eyed relish, how mustard gas would get into our lungs. This meant that we would have just two and a half minutes at most to fit the contraption over our face to save our lives. Armed with a whistle, like a race official at a dog track, he would then time us. In the event the Germans didn't use mustard gas this time - having decided that bombing from the air would cause us more discomfort. I owe the fact that I am still here to this as my lamentable efforts to get the mask on in the allotted time would have consigned me to an early oblivion.

Eventually the train, the steam puffer type, reached Derby. It was a revelation to us to discover that 'The North' was not just a vast wasteland after all, but had towns in it including the one we were decanted at i.e. Derby. Our first meeting point was the Town Hall, where we again lined up and numbers placed on our chests, by way of identification so that the families who had ordered us could see which children they were getting. Soon the families themselves were called in and began to look along the line of evacuees to claim their prize and cart him or her home. Their faces registered the whole gamut of responses from delighted through to disappointment to appalled, according to whether or not they liked the look of what they were getting. Altogether it seemed like a cross between a cattle market and an auction sale.

Our new home for the rest of the war was a house on the outskirts of Derby and was inhabited by a couple whose own daughter was married and had gone to live elsewhere. We were lucky in that they were kind and did not have young children at home to compare us unfavourably with. There were others who were not so lucky. The husband was a keen fisherman, the river Derwent flowed nearby and there were silver cups behind a glass case in the living room – which they called 'the best room'. The word 'lounge' had not yet come into general use except in the more exalted classes. I was to accompany the husband and his friends on Sunday mornings to fish in the Derwent. Many a tale was recounted about the 'one that got away' which always seemed to be bigger than any of those that were caught.

Fitting into a new home with temporary parents was a surprisingly smooth transition, but starting a new school was not.

First there was the accent. Many and loud were the heated assertions in the playground the we 'sootheners' had the wrong one. Why did they say 'coop of tea' instead of 'cap of tea' was only one of the issues hotly disputed? Neither side would give way on any of this item of fierce regional pride and the matter was always concluded – though never decided – by a fight with anything up to a dozen joining in. This was when I discovered that England is a country divided by a common language.

Another major problem was the Derby children's complete misunderstanding of what the word 'evacuee' meant. They were convinced that we had been sent out of London on account of some minor criminal activity on our part. What did you do? This was the question often shot at us, and great was the disappointment when we were not able to produce examples of lurid delinquency to explain our appearance in 'The North'. The experience was especially galling to the cockney children of the dockland area of the East End, whose only fault was to live near the Port of London docks and, as in many cases, to have been bombed out of their homes. Their contribution to the linguistic divide was not just their fists, which they deployed in a manner marvellous to behold, but an outpouring of language so colourful that some were sent home with a note to say that they would be allowed back into school only on condition of acceptable behaviour.

If Derby was expecting genteel decorum from East End children who had had a hard life, who had been bombed out and now were being teased in the playground, then Derby would be disappointed.

One ginger haired boy, one of Dickens legions of the 'great unsoaped', stood up in class and exclaimed 'F*** this for a lark', treated all present with the reverse V for victory gesture and walked out. He was later retrieved by the police having set out with a little bundle of belongings on the road leading out of Derby, which he imagined led all the way to London.

All in all there were lessons to be learnt from evacuation. The English language is a glorious dialectical muddle which is why we have a great literary heritage. We were able to take criticism on board and the real eye opener was that there actually was sentient life further north than Middlesex. Even trains travelled further up than that.

We returned home in the Spring of 1945 when the war ended, to the same primary school we had left a year earlier and to the same teachers who told us how lucky we were not to have been under Nazi occupation. Even the teasing about our accents was better than bombs. I have remembered their words ever since. In the cinema in Tottenham High Road film shots, just released by the government of the newly liberated death camps of Belsen and Auschwitz left us with a profound sense of both the sufferings of the victims and of our good fortune in being free.

Passwords and Passion

CHRIS MUTTON

I don't agree with much that Morrissey says these days but I do agree with him when he states 'There's more to life than books, you know. But not much more.'

My love of books and reading comes from being raised in a home where they were an integral part of family life as they were valued and used. My parents were readers as are my brother and I.

My dad insisted that we read the classics and so I am familiar with such works as Treasure Island, Lorna Doone, Robinson Crusoe and Uncle Tom's Cabin, but by far my favourite author was Enid Blyton. I remember Brer Rabbit being a favourite and I read all her fairy tales of magic shoes, cats, toys and, of course, fairies and elves - books which stretched my ever active imagination. I also loved The Milly Molly Mandy series written by Joyce Lankester Brisley. And then I discovered The Famous Five, Secret Seven and Adventure Books. I have lost count of the number of times I have read Five Run Away Together. As an adult it's easy to see the blatant racism and snobbery which is inherent throughout but I was blissfully unaware as a child that I was part of the working class problem where kidnapping and robbery were rife. I only saw the brave children overcoming all odds whilst camping or bike riding and learned the need for a password for almost every occasion. I loved and envied the picnics - especially the ginger beer, I also wondered about dripping sandwiches which seemed to be the fare of the aforementioned working class. Bless my mum, she bought me ginger beer - still one of my favourite drinks, made me a dripping butty and she and my father watched with great amusement as I took my first bite and heaved - and so I learned about the disappointments of life and that my beloved dad was not above saying 'I told you so'. One of my happiest childhood memories is of being taken to Queen's Park, by my mum, and sitting under a huge tree to have a picnic. And, just like ginger beer I still love picnics,

I think my dad worried that my reading habits were quite constrained. I'm not sure how old I was when I was taken to join the library. My dad was, I realise now, a great educator, I knew how important libraries were because they provided free reading materials for everyone. I also knew that the first free library had been started 'just down the road', I think the concept of Salford would have been outside my ken - the furthest I went was Walkden, a mile away from home. I still love going to the library and I'm sure it's because I was made to feel so important when I joined. I was told, by my dad, that he and mum had talked about it and decided that I was old enough to look after the books I could take out, and that it was very important that I did because other people would want to read them after me. I was duly taken to Little Hulton Library and introduced to the librarian, who was informed I was responsible enough to look after the books I would pick. I can also remember him taking the librarian to one side and asking if she could show me anything that was NOT Enid Blyton. And so *Paddington Bear,* by Michael Bond, entered my life. He brought the need to try a marmalade sandwich - which was on a par with the dripping, as far as I was concerned (I've never tried it since) and the obsessive need to read books in the order they are written began. I can remember the excitement of seeing all the books and being told I could choose more than one! I have never lost this feeling. As I got older I read, from the library, the entire series of books entitled 'The Young . . . ' which were children's biographies of people such as Mozart, Charles Dickens, Shakespeare and Helen Keller, there were many more - all read but I fail to remember the names of the others. The other series I remember were books on different careers, the one I remember was 'Hilary wants to be a librarian' but there were ones about the army, navy, teaching - whichever one I read was my career of choice for that week. I also remember dad taking me and helping choose books which would help with homework, possibly the most useful one was a book of Shakespeare plays in prose.

Alongside books were my weekly comics. I started off with one chosen by my mum, *Schoolgirl's Friend* but was allowed to have two when *Bunty* came out in 1958. These comics had tales of boarding school and ballet and magic toys and reinforced the awareness that passwords were needed! *Bunty* also had cutting out dolls on the back page which became another favourite pastime. At some stage of my reading development I became a fan of DC comics, Superman and Batman being my favourites. These were bought from Hennan's, a book stall/hut at the edge of Farnworth Market. There, new and second hand copies of books and comics could be bought and exchanged, money being knocked off the price of the new purchase when the old one was returned. This was on a par with choosing books at the library and trips to Farnworth were frequently requested. Luckily mum used to buy books from there so the request was usually granted. Inevitably, I suppose, I also discovered three new, to me, series of Enid Blyton: The Twins at Saint Clare's; Mallory Towers and The Naughtiest Girl. (You just can't keep a good author down!)

Christmas brought, bought books and annuals, the annuals representative of the comics my brother and I were reading at that time and for me a new Enid Blyton. Every year we received a book from my mum's brother and his wife in Australia, Uncle Len and Aunty Mary. To my disgust I always got a *Rupert Bear* whilst my brother got exciting adventure stories. Worse still, I had to write a thank you letter saying how much I liked it. One year though, I did receive a copy of Grimm's Fairy Tales, which I still have, which has the most grotesque illustrations I have seen and so for years, although I loved (and still do!) these stories I never liked that particular book - I don't think I ever got a book I was excited to receive from them, how sad.

When I was fifteen my dad bought me a copy of *Goldfinger* by Ian Fleming, I remember my mum queried the content and was it alright for me to read. He also took me to see the film, just me and him, a rare treat. It's still my favourite Bond film and book - and yes, I read them all, in order.

The next series I remember reading was the Denis Wheatley Roger Brook series followed by his novels of witchcraft and demonry. The first 'saucy' books I read were The Marianne Series by Juliette Benzoni, which had to stay hidden from my parents as they would not have approved! My mum eventually converted me to Catherine Cookson. To my dad's disgust I discovered Barbara Cartland and Georgette Heyer - I think he despaired that his efforts to steer me in **his** right direction had failed.

He needn't have worried; my taste in literature today is varied and eclectic. I think my favourite novels prove this. They are: Jane Eyre by Charlotte Bronte; Wuthering Heights by her sister Emily; Passage to India, E. M. Forster; Handmaid's Tale Margaret Atwood and The Grass is Singing by Doris Lessing. I also love James Patterson, Harlan Coben and Maeve Binchey and many more. I have recently discovered Cecilia Ahern, Michelle Paver and James Smythe - all very different genres. (If you like an excellently written ghost story - give Michelle Paver a try)

I'm so glad I was given the gift of loving books and reading and the ensuing escapism they bring. I have two regrets - one is that I haven't kept a book diary of every book I have read and the other is that it took me so many years to break my mum's rule that I had to finish every book I started. So many books, so little time!

1958 School Memories

ROSEMARY SWIFT

During late January/early February 1958, as a 10 year-old schoolgirl, along with my classmates I had stayed beyond the normal 4 pm end of school time for extra lessons as our 11+ examination was looming.

It was already dark outside as we pored over our mock Mathematics, English Language and IQ test papers. We were distracted by the classroom door opening and a nun coming in to whisper to Miss McCormack, which resulted in our head teacher clapping her hands for our attention and gravely saying: '*You need to go home at once, girls; there has been a disaster – Manchester United's plane has come down on their return from playing in Europe.*'

I cannot remember running home with any of the other girls, although I must have done. I was so focused as I crossed Every Street from Carruthers Street; Ancoats Library brightly lit up and beyond that the renowned Roundhouse, established 1895 to offer education and cultural opportunities to the local working poor.

But I was not turning right to visit the library which I loved doing on a weekly basis. I turned left and then right onto Russell Street, running, running, running though the mist as if my life depended on it. Over the humpbacked bridge where steam was rising as trains chugged below and passing by the streets all bearing the names of Victorian politicians, such as Orme and Roseberry. The main road, off which they run to the right and to the left, was Albert Street and when I reached Harcourt Street (the one before Rylance Street) I turned sharply right past the corner shop, then past Miss Pollitt's house, then past my maternal grandparents', Grandpop and Gran Lynch, house and then next door to them I ran into my own home bursting with the news that I thought I was going to impart to my parents and four brothers.

There was an eerie silence as I took in my family gathered about the table, attempting to eat their evening meal - of course they already knew! In fact, the streets had been so silent – everybody knew! The full extent of it was revealed over the following days but I will never forget that first notification.

My class was to report the following week or so to Ardwick High School (later renamed Ellen Wilkinson High School) to sit our 11+ exam of which 12 of us passed – a marvellous achievement for an inner city school. Three (including myself) went on to Notre Dame Convent High School, another three or four to Loreto High School and the remainder to St. Joseph's Technical School.

We girls that had passed the 11+ had the privilege of holding a banner ribbon when our Parish of St. Anne's, Ancoats took part in the Whit Walks. It was such a large parish (which my parents and their siblings had also attended) that we had our own resident Brass Band and Pipe Band which we proudly marched behind, alternating each year with the boys school. That particular year of 1958 we girls followed our Pipe Band which always seemed more exotic than the Brass Band.

So although 1958 was a landmark school year for me – full of hope and excitement - I can never forget it being tinged with sadness at its start.

Tell It Like It Is.

COLIN BALMER

From time to time when my six children were at home, I found myself in charge of all domestic arrangements. These occasions could be minor hospitalisation or well-earned holidays away for my enviably capable wife. Many of these circumstances produced what our family call 'adventures'. Without our happy-go-lucky acceptance of life's challenges these adventures could be reinterpreted as disasters, but the regularity of these events breeds a family sang-froid, sometimes misunderstood as indifference.

On one such tour of responsibility, the eldest four boys had been dispatched to school, leaving me at home to manage the still incontinent baby and my toddler daughter. All responsibilities fell on my willing, but domestically clueless, shoulders. I soon discovered that colours could migrate in a washing machine. My colour blindness prevented this becoming too much of a concern, although the neighbourhood grapevine buzzed with the colourful creation of a washing line bedecked in pink terry nappies – ironic in a house with five boys and even the girl well past the need for recyclable absorbent base layers. The roseate hue persisted even when my wife came back home, relieved that the washing line was mostly out of sight in the back garden, but more so that the washing had been done.

The feminine half of the pre-school dynamic duo features in her own contribution to the Cameron family history. I was, again, the responsible adult for a shopping expedition, a buggy-push some half mile to the precinct in Swinton. We had travelled at as fast a pace as my three year old daughter could manage for about five minutes when she started to lose speed. I urged her to hurry.

'My knickers are falling down!' she explained.

Her underwear having been adjusted, we continued for another four or five minutes and once more she started to lag.

'My knickers are falling down again,' she explained with that unique frustrated stamp of a girl.

I realigned the offending garment, giving her as much comfort as I could manage in my frustrated hurry to get the shopping done and out of the way.

The third time lowering of the linen came just a few hundred yards from the precinct and the realisation came to me.

'I'm sorry, darling. I think I must have dressed you in Mummy's knickers this morning.'

(An easy mistake to make where daughter's and mother's have a similar paucity of pink material. And, in a hurry, who checks labels anyway?)

'Silly Daddy. That's why they keep falling down,' was her knowledgeable response.

The shopping went as well as I could have hoped until we emerged onto the concourse among the many shops. In a crystal clear declaration, my daughter showed how knowledge had benefitted her understanding of the continuing problem with the announcement to the attentive throng.

'Daddy, Mummy's knickers are coming down again.'

Growing Up Fishing

STELLA SILVERSTEIN

One of my favourite memories growing up was going fishing and/or crabbing with my parents. My parents started taking me fishing with them when I was maybe six or seven, when we were living in Bermuda, and this continued until my early teens after we moved to the USA. What was unusual about this was both my parents liked going fishing, and it was considered a family outing. I don't remember my sister liking it very much though, or maybe she was too young when my parents started taking me out. She is five and a half years younger than I am.

I remember my dad took me to the fishing shop to find a new fishing pole and showing me how to bait the hook just right. We kept a bucket next to us with water for the fish, my mother liked her fish very fresh and kept them alive until right before cooking. I remember the crabs scurrying around their cages, and my mom explaining to me that blue crabs tasted the best. I remember the big family dinners, where the table was covered in newspaper, with the nut crackers next to me on one side for the crabs, the fish with my mom's vinegar and garlic sauce on the other and a heaped plate of rice in the middle to eat with it all. Catching your food, and then eating it was a main event growing up.

I loved growing up on an island. The warm salty winds blew in my face, the sharp smell of the water hitting my nose every morning when I woke up, and the sunny days where we ran around on the grass or the sand evoked fond memories my entire adult life. Bermuda is a tiny island in the middle of the Atlantic Ocean. It is far away from the continental shelf which surrounds the North American Atlantic Coast. The American shelf extends up to fifty miles, whereas a couple miles off the Bermuda coast, you are right in the middle of the deep sea and the ocean floor is a very long way away. Many people go deep sea diving off the coast of Bermuda due to its waters also being very clear. I loved snorkelling in the crystal clear waters.

One of my favourite memories about going fishing with my parents was the one day they took me deep sea fishing. We were looking for tuna fish that day. Tuna fish can only be caught in the deep ocean and they are huge. That day was a blustery windy day, the waves slapped the sides of the small boat we were on, and I remember the big fishing lines. I loved fresh tuna fish steaks, and to this day, they are one of my favourite fish to eat. Nothing tastes as good as freshly caught and sliced tuna steak cooked outside on a charcoal grill.

I was about 10 that day we went fishing for tuna. The boat rocked unsteadily on the ocean, the waves slapped the sides and some even made it over the top and splashed the deck of the boat. Back and forth, back and forth, the little boat moved jauntily over the water. Splosh splash went the waves over the sides as they happily danced with the boat. She was a merry white little boat, and I could tell she was well loved by her captain. My mother looked at me in absolute misery as she hung over the side, losing all the contents of her stomach on a pretty regular basis and also feeding the fish. My dad stood to the side of her, rubbing her back every so often, looking at me to make sure I was ok, and then looking around the boat watching everyone prepare the fishing lines. I was so excited. I rolled my walk across the desk, rolling with the ship, never once losing my balance. My sandwich was in one hand and my drink was in the other. I don't remember where my siblings were at the time, but I don't think either one was with us. I loved being on the open ocean, feeling the salt gently bit at my face and the sun hiding behind the clouds. I remember wearing a light jacket and my favourite pair of jeans that day, the wind made it a little chilly, although it wasn't cold. I was born to be a sailor. The ocean stretched out for miles and miles around us, miles of endless blue waves tipped with little brushes of white, and there was neither land nor another boat in site. I felt so alive that day. My mother looked at me, shook her head, and turned back to put her face over the side of the boat.

My father gently tapped me on the shoulder and pointed to the captain. He was straining with the massive fishing line. Maybe he finally caught a big tuna fish?!? There were already the small fish in nets around us. Some of the other passengers who were actually fishing were lucky enough to catch some. My father was too busy rubbing my mother's back, my mother was too busy losing her stomach, and I was happily eating my sandwich. I don't remember anyone in my family holding a fishing pole that particular day for more than a few minutes. The captain though, he looked really busy fishing. I caught my breath and forgot to chew. I was so caught up waiting to see what the captain was fighting with at the end of that massive fishing pole. It was attached to the ship, way too big for a person to actually hold it. There was a small handle and spool attached to the side of the fishing pole. This type of fishing is called trolling and is considered the ultimate sport-fishing challenge. I didn't know this at the time, I was only 10. All I knew that day was the captain was smiling and laughing as the fishing pole was bent almost straight back from the boat because whatever was on the other side of the line did not want to end up on the deck at our feet.

The fish that landed that day on the boat was only about 15 kilos. For a tuna fish that is about an average catch. It was still a great day.

Youth Hostelling

VERONICA SCOTTON

With all the arrogance of youth, I along with my cousin and my two friends decided that we would not be seen dead at the school camp in the Lake District. We decided instead to go youth hosteling.

With my rucksack loaded with clothes, shoes and all the other paraphernalia considered necessary by a 16 year old and £10 in my purse we prepared to go.

The holiday began the day before because Ann, my friend, lived in a children's home and since we were going to catch an early bus we stayed the night. How I envied her. She had her own bedroom, she had spends every week and she knew her rights. I couldn't imagine arguing with my mum, she was the boss and our daily lives were ruled by what mood she was in.

The next morning we caught the bus into Manchester and the coach to Keswick. When we arrived, staggering under the weight of our necessities, we found that the hostel was full. We hadn't even considered that possibility and went into a cafe to buy a drink while we decided what to do. Then it started raining. We got out a map to look how far it was to the next hostel, just as Mr Burke, the Deputy Head from our school, walked past and spotted us. He told us to follow him back to camp, where he gave us a bin bag each, then told us that, apart from underwear, we only really needed one spare set of clothes in case the ones we were wearing got wet. We would be glad of his advice by the end of the week. He persuaded us that it was too late to start walking to the next hostel and let us sleep under an awning stretched between two tents With only a sleeping bag between us and the ground it was cold and uncomfortable, but somehow we slept.

It was only when Tricia, the most sensible one of us four, decided to work out how much money we had available to spend each day, that I realised I had lost my purse. We tripped into the Police Station and reported the purse missing. The Bobby on the desk asked me where I last remembered having it (in the cafe), how much was in it (£10 less my bus fare and the price of a cup of tea), and what colour, I was as dizzy then as I am now, and couldn't remember. He produced the purse from under the desk and told us to go back to the cafe and thank the owner.

We set off walking to Helvellyn just as the heavens opened, within minutes we were soaked. When a car stopped and asked us where we were heading and did we want a ride, we didn't hesitate, although I'm sure that was one of the warnings we had received from the teachers on camp - 'under no circumstances get into a stranger's car'. The lady car driver chatted to us and stopped half way to buy us tea and biscuits at a very fancy hotel. Goodness knows what the manager thought about the four bedraggled, Salford girls dripping rainwater all over his carpets, but the lady was apparently a regular customer and so he didn't complain. She even encouraged us to fill our pockets with the sugar cubes from the table.

We arrived at the hostel hours earlier than we had predicted, and of course it didn't open until the late afternoon, so we dumped all our belongings on the doorstep and went to explore the town. The rain had stopped and we picnicked in a park on rations we had brought from home and imagined that we were on the adventure of a lifetime. It never occurred to us that someone might steal our rucksacks which contained all of our possessions. The Youth Hostel was basically a long low shed with girls' bedrooms at one end and boys' at the other. In the middle was a bedroom for a warden. He was there to stop testosterone filled youths practicing their sexuality on the pure lily white girls at the other end. As we sat on our pyjamas, excitedly recalling our day's adventure and playing cards, the warden came into our dormitory and asked if anyone of us fancied a game of chess in his room, I innocently set off to follow him. Fortunately for me, my friends were more worldly wise and explained that 'playing chess' was a euphemism.

It was a holiday of our dreams, after our successful car trip on the first day, we no longer attempted to walk, but stood at the side of the road and thumbed lifts, climbing into cars, vans and lorries without a care. We took a boat ride on Coniston Water, daringly dipping our fingers in the water, in which we were sure there were man-eating fish, after all, Donald Campbell's body hadn't been found after his crash earlier in the year. We pretended to be American practising the accent on anyone who would listen. I'm sure no-one was fooled.

Armed only with a road map, we somehow travelled the Lake District and got home safely. I now pocket my phone before I leave the house, just in case I need to contact someone, or they need to contact me, or, in case I need to google some information, or use Apple Pay to buy something. Perhaps I might want to take a photo or check the date of an appointment or use the PictureThis App to identify a plant or tree. I might get bored and listen to music, play a game, count my steps or make a comment on Facebook. However did we manage in 1967?

Holidays

CHRIS MUTTON

Holidays, when I was little, began with a two hour journey, my brother and I sitting on the knees of our parents and our one, shared, suitcase stored under the stairs of the X70 double decker bus: Destination Blackpool!

We always stayed at a guest house in Bispham, a quiet suburb, just north of Blackpool, and close to a Catholic Church - very important for my mother, in fact the first question she asked was 'Where is the church?' followed by, 'What time is Mass?' This duly taken care of, the holiday could begin!

During the day, my brother and I played on the beach with our new buckets and spades, carefully chosen from one of the sea front shops - in those days it was unheard of for children to have an opinion, let alone express it, and we were usually discouraged from 'wants' so I can still remember the excitement of being allowed to pick our own, even though we'd had long debates for weeks before about what colour we were going to have. This of course would lead to arguments about who 'bagged' the best colour first, but was usually solved by one having first pick for the bucket and one for the spade - usually after the threat of not getting anything if we didn't stop arguing. If we were lucky, we got a small packet of paper flags on thin sticks to go on top of our sand castles.

Once on the beach the careful job of building the best and biggest sand castle would begin. On completion we would walk down to the water's edge to fill our buckets with sea water and carefully carry them back to put into the moat, never fully getting that it would soak into the sand. We never quite got it, either that my father hadn't been quite honest with us when he said we could dig to Australia - but I suspect it kept us busy for the duration of our time on the beach. I can still smell the sea and feel the seaweed under my feet. I never liked Punch and Judy but loved the donkey rides. Donkeys have another evocative smell that takes me back to childhood.

The beach wasn't the only source of entertainment. Walks along The Promenade, where the green and cream corporation trams were a source of excitement - and potential danger, we were warned when we walked too near the tram lines. We were also given instructions to 'breathe deep' to get the sea air in our lungs and to make our way to *The Foxhall Hotel* if we got separated - a standard procedure in the days prior to mobile phones. Near to this pub was my favourite attraction - Fairyland! To a child whose head was filled with the contents of her beloved Enid Blyton books about fairies, elves and sprites, this was indeed paradise on earth. My Dad and I would sit in little cars that went round a section of tunnels, each showing a different magical woodland scene to the side.

We visited Stanley Park, with its large boating lake and playground containing a large slide and umbrella roundabout and lots of grass to run on. There was an open air paddling pool,which we could only go in if 'we remembered the towels', although one stormy year the sea flooded onto the walkway at the top of the beach in Bispham, and my brother and I spent a merry morning dancing and splashing in it. We played crazy golf - and thought we were very sophisticated as we 'did a round'. Another annual treat was to go to see the man making rock and find out how they managed to get the word Blackpool exactly in the middle. To this day I love pink rock and am immediately transported back to the small backstreet workplace behind the Promenade when I smell the peppermint. If it rained we were treated to Madame Tussauds where we viewed the wax figures in wonder - especially the one of Ann Boleyn which, we all agreed, was an exact replica of my favourite Auntie Ann!

Some things we weren't allowed: I always wanted to go in one of the horse drawn carriages that took lucky (and wealthier) holiday makers down The Golden Mile -but the reply was always 'not today'. 'Kiss Me Quick' hats were a definite no as my mum thought they were 'common' but it seemed to me that everyone had one and looked very smart. As Catholics we weren't allowed to visit any of the many Gypsy Rose Lee tents, but oh how I wanted to see what was inside!

I don't remember the food we ate but I can remember the Candyfloss- huge wisps of twirled sugar that stuck to faces, hair, hands and all around our mouths. We always had a tray of shrimps from one of the many stalls along the promenade and at night time, on the walk back to the boarding house we stopped off at the same cafe, where I either had Campbell's vegetable soup in a cup - a rare treat because at home we only had homemade, or 'frothy' Horlicks (at home it was flat and really didn't taste as nice!). One year, when we got home, my mum collected tokens off the Horlicks packaging until we had enough to send off for a froth maker - a round sieve-like top on a long metal handle which was plunged up and down in the drink to make froth. On one holiday my Dad discovered Lipton's lemon tea - and was a fan of this drink until the day he died.

One year, whilst on holiday, we went to Fleetwood for the day, to see the fishing boats being unloaded. We had a fish dinner and then went to a Chinese Restaurant for tea! This was our first 'foreign' meal. However, it's memorable, not because of the food, I have no idea what we ate, but because my brother and I found a shilling under the plate and took it. Outside the restaurant we showed it to our parents and didn't understand why we were in trouble - but that's how we learned what leaving a tip meant.

My mother loved the theatre and so the second job of the holidays, after a trial walk to the church, was to book the shows we would see on the first four nights. In those days Blackpool

160

attracted many of the best acts of the day: Ken Dodd, Hilda Baker (and Our Eli); Val Doonican; Mark Wynter; Les Dawson and Charlie Drake are some of the stars I remember seeing on the stage of The Winter Gardens, with its indoor tropical plants and palm trees and the splendid Victorian Grand Theatre and the North and Central Piers.*

A night in The Tower meant, firstly, seeing the circus. Excitement mounted as we joined the long, long queue waiting to gain entrance to the, then, highest building in the UK (as we were told every year by Dad.) Staff wore very glamorous uniforms, including a Fez, which was very exotic in those days. Dad told us he'd seen people wearing real ones in Egypt, where he was stationed during the war. He used to tell us tales of camels, pharaohs, pyramids and mummies and take us to Bolton Museum to see the artifacts, including actual mummies thus giving us a love of all things Egyptian, so to own a fez would have been wonderful, but sadly this never happened.

In the fifties animals were still to be seen and wondered over as we saw dancing horses and elephants, as well as the trapeze artists, who literally flew through the air, acrobats and of course the clowns causing mayhem at every interval. This was followed by a visit to The Tower Ballroom via the aquarium and one-arm bandit machines - where we stood obediently and watched mum spend her carefully hoarded penny coins. When she was younger, Mum was an avid ballroom dancer and she loved to sit and watch the couples gliding by, doing a waltz, foxtrot or quickstep. When I was a little older we would dance these together. My Dad had spondylosis of the spine so could no longer dance but he loved organ music and was in his element listening to the great organ in The Tower Ballroom. My brother and I liked the lemonade and bag of Smiths Crisps - once we'd found the little blue bag of salt and sprinkled it over the contents. Everyone was happy, except for one year when, according to Mum, I ruined everything. It had rained through the day and my brother and I were bought a plastic mac - his was grey and mine was pink. I left mine under the seat where I had sat to watch the circus. We went back to look but it had gone. She shouted, I cried and my brother and I remember this happening to this day - I've never had a plastic mac since.

Our last night, Friday, was reserved for walking through the magical lights of The Illuminations. The entire promenade was lit up including The Tower. Lights were strung across the road and there were themed display lights of vegetables, musical instruments, and, my favourites, fireworks. Best of all was when the decorated trams went past - there was a rocket, a train and a yacht. We happily walked 'The Golden Mile' to finally end up at The Pleasure Beach, excited and mithering our parents as we worried that our favourite attraction might not be there - until we finally heard the loud bellows of The Laughing Policeman before we could see him. We were allowed chips but only after we'd been on the rides (so we wouldn't be sick). And, oh what rides there were! Some, we didn't go on but the sight of the lights and sound of the music of the rides such as the huge Pirate Swingboat, Ferris Wheel and Virginia Wheel, a spinning wooden roller coaster, added to the atmosphere. The Haunted Swing, Noah's Ark, Ghost Train and my favourite, The Caterpillar, were the 'big' rides we were allowed on along with the children's Safari Ride -where all the carriages were jungle animals and the small carousel with horses that went up and down as well as round and round and then the rides with a variety of miniature cars, buses and airplanes

If we were lucky Noddy's car would be empty. If it wasn't, we drove the bus, ringing the golden bell which hung from a piece of string over the driver's seat.. Finally it was The Mirror Maze, where we looked all different heights and widths, and then back to Bispham, on the tram, to see once more The Illuminations which ended at Squire's Gate - after the tableaux of children's stories and rhymes - Alice in Wonderland, Goldilocks and the Three Bears, The Grand Old Duke of York and his marching men , Humpty Dumpty continuously falling and Little Bo Peep losing then finding her sheep. Only once were we lucky enough to get on a decorated tram and sadly Dad was right, it was just an ordinary tram inside and wasn't as much fun riding in it as seeing it go past and waving to the driver.

We had other holidays. I remember staying in a caravan on a farm at Llandudno and Dad teaching us to say 'bore da' as we left the village shop - not a cultural move but rather a retaliation for their speaking Welsh suddenly as we entered. Another Welsh holiday was at The Robin Hood Holiday Camp in Rhyl in a chalet - one of many in rows upon rows. Strangely I don't remember many details of these other holidays, but when I visit steam train museums and take a deep breath I am instantly transported to a railway station, feeling the grit in my eye as I watch my dad speak to the train driver, which he did every time we went on one. I realise, as an adult, that he was checking we were about to board the correct train but as a child I firmly believed that Dad knew EVERY train driver and never doubted that we would arrive where we were meant to and that we would have a wonderful time.

The Winter Gardens and The Carousel on North Pier are Grade 2 listed. The Grand Theatre was saved from demolition and restored to its former glory after a campaign by The Nolan Sisters.

Last Story

COLIN BALMER

As I contemplated the three-legged cobbler's last in the Museum of Science and Industry, my mind drifted back to my childhood days in the nineteen fifties when 'make and mend' was the rule – not 'buy now, pay later'. I can almost hear Petula Clark singing, '*In the shoemaker's shop this refrain would never stop. As he tapped away...*'

Growing up in Wythenshawe shortly after the war, we weren't a well-off family by any means, but my parents, like the rest of the neighbourhood, always managed to make ends meet. The last was as commonplace a domestic DIY tool then as the power drill is today. In my mind's eye, I can picture my Dad employing self-taught skills to mending the family's footwear with the black cast iron triumvirate of anvils. He would explain through a mouthful of nails, how the tripod was used to hold the shoe while he nailed on the new sole and heel shapes, cut from a sheet of cow hide. He'd told us the largest was the anvil for men's shoes, the smaller foot-shaped platform was used for women's and the almost circular pedestal was used for heels.

A more imaginative mind than mine could, no doubt, create a biblical connection with Adam's rib and talk of soles as I consider the damaged last. Later in life, I absorbed some engineering and I realised how a design fault in the cast iron mould had resulted in a weaker rib on the lady foot, which is why this plate was often broken. Was it foundry chauvinism that made the distaff part the weaker or had some erstwhile cobbler swung his hammer more aggressively at his wife's sole? Consider this when next you see a last with apparently two small 'heel' plinths.

At times, when the weather permitted, we would forego proper leather soles and be satisfied with oilcloth, lino or even cardboard insoles. We were not the only kids with toes peeping through crocodile shoes with bull's eye soles - nor were we bothered. The weather was more clement as a kid and the sun always shone in those days – didn't it?

Nor was the last tucked away in a drawer between repairs. As kids, we were impressed at the weight of the last, which we knew would stop any door swinging in the gale-force drafts that used to cyclone round our homes in the days before central heating and double glazing. It really hurt if you dropped it on your foot. There was never any 'if' about that, gravity and retribution always drew heavy iron 'things-you-don't-play-with' towards your toe! It was the goal post that did not move. It was the extra hand when something needed holding down while the glue was setting. Until we grew into 19' frames and 26' wheels, it would be the ideal height as a bike stand. The poker would complement the last in an effective nut cracking duo. And woe betide any skulking burglar who thought the house was undefended and weaponless!

Even as I was raising my own family, the last saw service in shoe repairing. But now we had moved on through the age of the stick on sole. To make a good bond between the shoe and sole it was necessary to remove bubbles in the adhesive. The last made an ideal work holder for the shoe as I pushed or hammered the sole. The heels, however, always merited the additional security of half a dozen nails.

The last of the family (sic!) has now progressed another generation in its trade. My daughter-in-law is now using it to make bespoke soft leather pumps for her daughter and son. At this rate, will we ever see the last of the last?

Other SWit'CH Publications

My Life and Other Misadventures

ISBN 978-1-326-60665-7

By Alan Rick

A collection of humorous and poignant nostalgic reminiscences covering Alan's early school years in the war to national service in Egypt. Alan looks askance at the society of the day with a wry, knowing, smile.

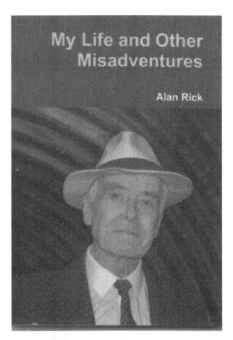

Switch On, Write On, Read On

ISBN 978-1-326-73048-2

Approx. 200 page the first showcase of the group's creativity. Containing nearly sixty humorous, whimsical, thought-provoking, ironic, and eclectic writing.

A Write Good Read

ISBN 978-0-244-73623-1

Tales from Swinton and Salford; the Wigan train and around the world drawing on the experiences and interests of the group. Modern telecoms and IT feature, so do the Ten Commandments and seven dwarfs. Historical pieces range from the industrial revolution to individual childhood memories.

Peterloo People

ISBN 978-0-244-18472-8

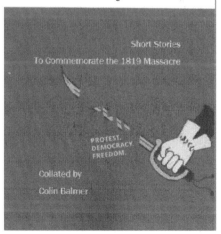

A potpourri of passions gives the reader the chance to walk in those shoes to the peaceful protest, the actions on the day and shameful reaction afterwards. But the focus is not only on the victims; the perspectives of the authorities and militia are treated with sympathy and criticism in due turn – and there's even a wry tale of hope and salvation for a pariah in the guise of a government spy.

167

The Taste of Teardrops

ISBN 978-0-244-26569-4

Novel by Judith Barrie.

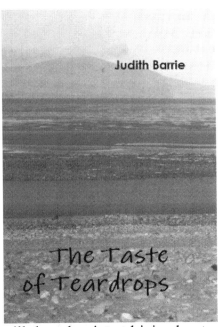

A gripping psychological thriller set in a sleepy seaside town on The Solway Firth. It's 1981 and a young woman settles into her cosy new home believing that she had found peace and tranquillity after a painful marriage break-up.

But there are mysteries. Who is the woman upstairs? And who is the irresistibly attractive man who visits her? Susan is unaware of the nightmare of pain and deceit he will draw her into, driving her to the very edge of her sanity.

The Big Switch

ISBN : 9798644090433

A collection of short stories in large print format for readers with a visual impairment like Macular Degeneration or Glaucoma.

'The Big Switch' is a compilation of extracts from some of the group's previously published works. It is designed for easy reading with a font design developed by RNIB.

Printed in Great Britain
by Amazon

55378909R00106